CRYSTAL CRAFT

How to choose, use, and activate your crystals, with 25 creative projects to display and wear

NICOLE SPINK

STERLING ETHOS
New York

CONTENTS

Introduction

Crystal Craft is a practical guide that I hope will inspire you to live a more conscious and empowered life. Not only will the 25 projects in this book show you how to create some beautiful and powerful objects to wear or display at home, crafting in itself can also be a very mindful and nourishing activity.

Surrounding yourself with beautiful things is a natural mood-booster. It is no secret that having fresh flowers in your home provides a great feel-good effect, and the same goes for crystals. They are lovely to look at and we are naturally drawn to them. Bringing crystals into your home environment, or wearing them, can have a hugely positive impact on your life. Crystals can help us feel more confident, relaxed, positive, and healthy.

Crystals can also help us to face challenges confidently and to connect and understand our deeper emotions. In addition, they can support our creative practices, balance our energy fields, and much more. The more we appreciate and understand how to connect with them, the more magick crystals can bring to our lives.

Crystal energy is a very personal experience. Crystal craft means choosing the crystals that speak to you for each project, which ensures that everything you create will be entirely personal and unique to each situation. Crafting will take you on a journey to connect with who you truly are, and nobody has the answers except you. Crystals can only show you what is already within you.

I hope you enjoy the projects in this book and learn something new about crystals. Whether you stick to the projects I created or simply use them as a starting point to create your own concepts, I am excited to guide you in a creative awakening as you bring the power of crystals into your life.

Getting Started with Crystals

Much like plants, crystals are alive, and they radiate subtle energies that we can sense. When we place crystals in a room, or use them or wear them, we are inviting their energy to connect with ours. Crystals can infuse our lives with an element of magick. Not to be confused with stage magic, the word "magick" refers to the conscious creation of our own reality with unseen forces using intention and sacred rituals. This book is a guide to help you to connect with crystals in your own way and become a crystal keeper.

Crystals have been regarded as sacred, mystical, and protective for thousands of years, and they can teach us how to connect more deeply with ourselves, with the people in our lives, and with our creative energy. Our ancestors knew so much about the natural world: crystals, astronomy, herbs, rituals, and the natural cycles of the earth were as natural a part of life to them as coffee and smartphones are to us. Now we are beginning to reconnect with this ancient wisdom. Crystal energy is subtle, though it can be powerful. Crystals are not a cure or a quick fix for the challenges we face in life. Instead, they are a tool that we can use to turn the turbulent times into opportunities for transformation. They guide and support us to help us feel aligned, healthy, grounded, and confident; they have taught me so much and continue to do so every day.

When you have a crystal, it is important to be aware that you are holding an ancient piece of the earth, and appreciate that the crystal you are holding, whatever it is, has been through so much before it came to you. Crystals are minerals that have been subjected to immense pressure and changes in environment to transform them into the beautiful structures that we enjoy.

I would recommend that, whether you are new to crystals or already have a large collection, you start keeping a journal to record your experiences with your crystals. When you start connecting with different crystalline energies, this will be very helpful for you to understand how different crystals are affecting you. For example, if you set

"Crystals are living beings at the beginning of creation."
— Nikola Tesla

an intention with a particular crystal to support you in a time of change and then you start to notice a lot of changes but can't understand why, you may find it helpful to track when you set your intentions and started to connect with different energies. Fine-tuning your senses and being clear with your intentions will help you become more aware of what you are creating in your life. As you connect more and more with crystals, your sensitivity to their energy will increase.

We all have different life experiences and crystals work in unique ways for each of us. You might experience a feeling of warmth when you hold a particular crystal, or it could be a color that comes to mind, or a vision or sensation. Always trust that the right crystals will find you when you need them, and that there is no right or wrong way to use them. It is simply a process of developing your connection to them and becoming aware of which crystals can help you in each moment or phase of your life.

Sourcing Crystals Ethically

Crystals are not currently listed as a fair-trade product, so, as a buyer and keeper of crystals, it is very important to find out where a crystal comes from before you buy it. Consider that, in some countries, laborers who mine for crystals may be underpaid and subject to very poor working conditions, while mining is often an environmentally destructive practice. Even if the ecological implications don't concern you, you may want to consider the energetic impact this has on the crystals and the energy they are bringing into your life. More and more companies are becoming aware of ethical practices and avoiding selling crystals that have come from unethical mining. Be sure to find out as much as possible about exactly where the crystals came from, which mine, and how the seller can ensure their crystals are fairly traded.

Crystals and other items you can include in your crafting projects can also be found in nature. If you visit the coast, you could explore the beach for shells, washed-up sea glass—or even actual crystals! When crystals come to you in this way, it feels even more special, as though they have been gifted by the earth. Shells and sea glass carry the energy of the ocean, which some people can feel when they hold them. Always ask before you take anything; talk to the crystals and nature and only ever take what you need. Be mindful of the equilibrium of nature and give thanks and offerings to ensure balance and harmony.

When buying crystals, it's easy to be overwhelmed by all the sparkling colors, but put the effort in to ensure you're getting the best quality materials, and make sure you are buying a crystal because your heart and body really feel a connection to it, rather than because you're attracted to its beauty or just think you need another crystal in your collection. Over time, you will begin to notice the ease with which crystals come into your life at the perfect moment.

Keeping Crystals

Crystals vibrating at their natural frequency will be glowing: not physically shining but radiating their energy. Over time, and with practice, you will start to sense when crystals are happy. Just like us, they have an aura that we can sense. There is no one right way to cleanse crystals; it is a personal process and you can change the way you cleanse your crystals at any time. As a guide, bear in mind that crystals have come from deep within the earth's crust, and they love anything that connects them back to the earth!

When you bring a new crystal home, the first thing you should do is cleanse it in your preferred way to ensure it is clear and ready to connect with your energy. It could have traveled halfway across the world and been handled by a lot of people before it got to you, so it is important to give it some care before you get started.

First, make sure you feel calm, grounded, and clear. Begin by breathing in for a count of four and out for a count of eight, allowing your body and mind to soften and relax. Connect to your heart space (the most powerful energy center we have in the body)—you may wish to place a hand on your heart to do this. Tune in to your body, your heart, and the physical sensations you can feel. As you inhale, fill yourself up with pure light and visualize your heart's energy glowing and radiating from your chest as it expands, filling your whole body with beautiful pink light—or any other color that makes you feel good. You may wish to call upon spiritual guidance from your higher self, gods, goddesses, spirit animals, guides—anything that helps you to connect to your power and presence. Feel the present moment deeply and dedicate this time and space to your intention, yourself, your connection, and your light. You are now ready to cleanse your crystals, using any of the techniques on the following pages or techniques of your own design.

Water

Before cleansing with water, check that your crystals are suitable for immersion. Soak crystals in purified salt water overnight, rinse them in a freshwater stream, or try taking them for a cleanse in the ocean once in a while. After soaking, rinse the salt water off with clean, pure water. If you use a glass bowl to soak your crystals, you may also wish to place the bowl on a grid or sacred geometric pattern to help the energies to rebalance and align.

Smoke

Cleansing with sage, palo santo, cleansing herbs or incense are all great ways to bathe your crystals in purifying smoke. Light your chosen wood or herbs and hold the crystal above the smoke. Visualize the smoke cleansing and purifying the crystal.

Sound

Sound is one of the most effective and sustainable ways to cleanse crystals. Try playing certain frequencies (such as 528hz), which you can find online, or create sound using a singing bowl, a drum, bells, or your voice! Chanting or singing the word *Aum* will help clear your mind and bring you into the present moment, while simultaneously cleansing your crystals.

Earth

Place crystals in soil for a few days when you get new ones to "earth" and ground their energy. You can also bury crystals in your garden or a forest and dig them up again after a day or two. I like to place them in the soil with my plants at home so they can rebalance together. Set your intention for Mother Earth to cleanse the crystals, and ask permission to take them back before you dig them up again.

Moonlight

Every month we have a natural opportunity to cleanse and charge crystals with energy from the full moon. Place your crystals outside on the earth or on a natural surface for a full-moon bath. You can also do this by placing them on a moonlit windowsill.

Visualization

Visualize your crystal being filled with pure white light and any energy that may have got stuck to it (anything that is not its natural frequency) washing away and being transformed into pure white light. Intention is everything: merely stating an intention to cleanse a crystal has already started the process.

How often?

This will vary for each crystal and depend on how often you wear it or where it is placed/stored. If you wear a crystal every day and are traveling a lot in public places or surrounded by a lot of external energy (such as WI-FI, other people, computers, etc.), then you may want to make it a ritual to cleanse them once a week. I like to connect cleansing my crystals with the moon cycles. Energetically, a full or new moon can be a supportive time to tune in and cleanse ourselves and our crystals.

Storing Crystals

It is really important to be mindful of how you store your crystals. Don't just throw them into the back of a drawer to get lost, damaged, or broken. Respect them: wrap them in a soft cloth and keep them safe when you are not using them. If they are on display, take care that they don't get too much sunlight, and clean them if they seem a bit dusty. You will notice the difference in how your crystals look and feel when you take care of them.

Crystal Intentions

Connecting to a crystal is a way to develop your unique relationship with it. Every crystal has its own essence and meaning, and when you consciously decide to connect to a crystal, it can energetically support and guide you with your intention. Begin by connecting with yourself, as you would to cleanse your crystals. Hold your crystal to your heart or a particular part of your body, or in your hand. Speak your intentions into the crystal. Ask the crystal to connect with you and share any messages, insights, and wisdom that are important for you in this moment. Feel free to find your own way: setting an intention is your personal ritual to connect with your crystal.

Setting intentions with crystals is not compulsory, but I recommend it to increase your connection. When I first started to buy crystals, I just had them in my room and appreciated them being there. Later, I started wearing crystals and appreciating them even more, but it was still only after a year of wearing my favorite amethyst talisman that I became aware of how alive and powerful this crystal was. I began to cleanse it, hold it during meditation, and really connect to it. I started to feel more connected and sense the personality of the crystal and I could tell when it needed to be cleansed.

Choosing Crystals

When you are deciding which crystal to buy, use, or craft with, always trust your intuition. Which crystal stands out to you? Do you notice a particular color or sensation, or does a particular crystal just feel good? Tune into a crystal's energy by holding it in your hand. Sometimes you can sense if a crystal is the right one for you just by looking at a photo of it. Trust that whichever crystal you are drawn to has something to share with you in this moment or period of your life.

Each crystal has a different energy: this is dependent on its unique molecular structure, where it was formed geographically in the earth and how it came to you. Each of these factors affects how a crystal will feel when you hold it. Scientists have discovered that crystals contain an electrical charge called *piezoelectricity*. This electrical charge is emitted from a crystal when it is pressed—that is, when you hold it in your hand. You ignite and switch on a crystal's energy when you connect to it. When we wear any crystal, it can strengthen and expand our energy field or *aura*.

Crystals come in many natural shapes and sizes; tumbled, clustered, pointed, flat, rough, smooth, and everything in between! Crystals don't always have to be beautiful; rough and unattractive stones can be the greatest teachers of strength, change, and endurance. A crystal's story is told by its appearance and feel. The ones used in the projects in this book are a guide, but you can be as creative as you like. When starting a crystal craft project, try to select crystal shapes that complement the project you are working on.

The experience you have with crystals will be unique to you. A crystal that is grounding for another person might not be grounding for you, and this can also change over time. It's important to stay present with which crystals you feel drawn to in each moment.

Over the page, you'll find 11 crystals I recommend for getting started.

AMETHYST – Radiating a soft, sweet energy, amethyst is calming for busy minds and can be helpful during meditation and when you want to unwind. Additionally, it can help stimulate your creative flow.

CITRINE – A happy crystal, stimulating feelings of joy and confidence. When you buy citrine, be aware that a lot of pieces sold as citrine are actually heat-treated amethyst. Genuine citrine is often a very light yellow, whereas heat-treated amethyst is usually golden yellow.

HEMATITE – The core of the earth is iron, and this crystal has the same mineral properties. Holding a piece of this crystal can help connect our energy more deeply to the earth. It will help the heart and lower chakras stay balanced and grounded.

CARNELIAN – A crystal for courage, optimistic energy, creativity, and confidence. This reddish-orange crystal can help support the sacral chakra (see page 20), creating balance and flow for sexual energy.

QUARTZ – A high-vibrational and stimulating crystal. It amplifies the energy of other crystals or energies around it. Clear quartz encourages clarity and is great for crystal beginners. Any variety of quartz will have a high and energizing effect so if you need to feel calm and grounded, stay away from it and choose a darker-colored crystal such as hematite.

LABRADORITE – Often used by shamans for healing and protection, labradorite is a transformation crystal. It can support times of transition, bring out our inner magick and enhance our connection to our higher self.

SELENITE – Radiating a high-vibrational, pure, and clear energy, not only does selenite keep its own energy clean, it also helps to cleanse and balance other energies, and can be used to cleanse other crystals, a room, or your aura. Hold a piece around your body when you feel you need to rebalance.

ROSE QUARTZ – A pink variety of quartz, these crystals can help us connect more deeply to our hearts and offer harmonious and nurturing energy. Their energy encompasses self-love, compassion, and nurturing feminine energy.

SHUNGITE – A grounding and powerful detoxifying energy that can help you to feel calm and clear. Ideal for protecting against electromagnetic frequencies and for purifying water.

SMOKY QUARTZ – A variety of quartz that ranges in color from light gray to dark brown. A balancing crystal that can help with grounding and emotional stability, although, as a variety of quartz it can still feel energizing.

FLUORITE – Comes in a variety of colors but is most commonly green, blue, purple, or a rainbow mixture. Helpful for reprogramming emotional patterns and has a gentle, calming feel for the mind and upper chakras. It has a powerful but grounding energy.

There are certain crystals that contain traces of metals, such as copper, which may cause a skin irritation. These include malachite and labradorite. Some crystals are more porous and shouldn't be submerged in water—for example, kyanite, fluorite, and selenite. They can become soft and break easily. Typically, stones ending with the suffix "ite" should not be kept in or near water. Always check if a crystal or metal agrees with your skin before wearing it or using it to infuse anything that will come into contact with your skin.

A Guide to Chakras

Different colors of crystals resonate with certain parts of our bodies, which can be broken down into energy centers called "chakras." Chakras are a very important part of many spiritual practices, especially Hinduism and Buddhism. The seven main chakras run along our spine. They are:

- ROOT: Red. Center for grounding and connection to the earth, and our sense of safety.

- SACRAL: Orange. Center for co-creation, passion, creative energy, and optimism.

- SOLAR PLEXUS: Yellow. Center for "gut instinct" and feeling happy, confident, and joyful, along with a sense of self-esteem.

- HEART: Green or light pink. Our most powerful energy center, for unconditional love, self-love, compassion, and fulfillment.

- THROAT: Blue. Center for expression, the bridge between our minds and hearts, expression of our truth.

- THIRD EYE: Violet or purple. Center for self-awareness, spiritual power, and divine connection. Activated through meditation.

- CROWN: White or violet. Center for spirituality, connection to the universe, and fulfillment.

When all our chakras are vibrating in a balanced and healthy way, we feel peaceful, safe, creative, and confident in ourselves. Placing crystals of the appropriate colors on relevant areas of the body can be a way to engage with the energy in that area. An example would be placing a red or very dark-colored crystal near the base of your spine to balance your root chakra.

Lots of different things can throw our energy off-center, from tricky encounters with other people to longer-term stress or illness. Understanding energy within our bodies and how different crystals can support us is a self-empowering approach to living a sustainable, healthy, and balanced life.

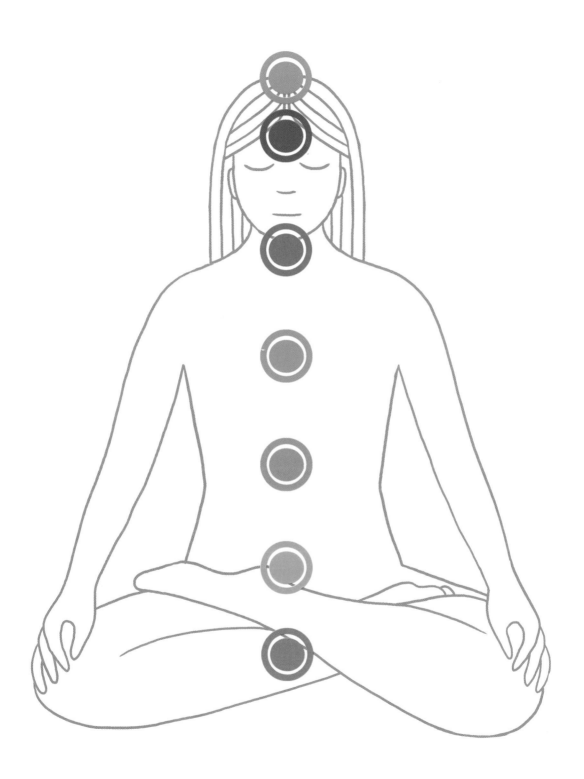

Conscious Crafting

Conscious crafting takes the practice of mindfulness (or mind empty-ness) and combines it with the hands-on experience of creating something. Crafting with crystals is an amazing way to connect with your mind, body, and soul. Crafting in this engaged, mindful way can teach us many things that we can take into our daily lives. In our relationships and our work, we are always creating and learning something. You might begin to see, for example, how making a necklace (and enjoying the process) can actually help you learn how to slow down and have deeper conversations and connections in other areas of your life. Crafting teaches us to slow down, be present, and really feel what we are doing, without feeling guilty for taking time to engage in creative pursuits purely for the pleasure of it.

Each project in this book has been broken down into easy-to-follow steps with illustrations as a guide. Enjoy the process, enjoy each moment (even when things don't work out), and discover that there is learning in everything—not just when we get it "right."

Cultivating a mindful daily practice will greatly enhance your connection and sensitivity to crystal energy. Centering yourself and practicing presence and reverence as part of daily life makes the simplest tasks more meaningful. You can practice waking up and starting your day by writing down things you feel grateful for—anything from your warm, cozy bed to your family or job—and focusing on the feeling of appreciation rather than what you think sounds right. When you make your morning tea or coffee, imagine you are infusing your drink with your intentions for the day ahead: what would you like to infuse your day with—creativity, energy, courage, joy? You could start a meditation or yoga practice. Just ten minutes in the morning over an extended period of time can dramatically shift your vibration, increase your sense of overall well-being, and help you feel inspired, more present, and more connected to your spirit.

Get in the habit of asking yourself regularly,

how am I feeling right now? Check in with your energy levels, your emotions, and the feelings in your body. Emotions (which are different energies in motion) are not good or bad. They are simply lighter and denser vibrations. When you start to recognize the vibrational nature of everything, you can better understand yourself (internally) and your life experiences (externally). This will help you to notice when you may need to change the crystals you have around you.

The more you work with crystals, the more you will develop your awareness of and connection to their subtle energies. Start slowly and always trust your intuition with which crystal you feel drawn to. As you work through the projects in this book, try to bring that mindfulness into your crafting: think about the reasons you were drawn to your chosen crystal, your reasons for making the piece you have chosen to make, and be conscious of the play of your emotions.

Tools and Materials

Most of the items used to make these projects are easy to obtain from good craft or DIY shops. Along with your chosen selection of crystals and crystal beads, you will need:

Scissors
Tape measure
Round-nose jewelry pliers
Flat-nose jewelry pliers
Small wire cutters
Glue gun
Waxed polyester thread (such as Linhasita) or
    0.5mm hemp cord
3mm (1/8in) recycled cotton cord
0.4mm (26 gauge), 0.5mm (24 gauge), and
    0.8mm (20 gauge) copper and silver wire

A NOTE ON WIRE
Metals have energetic properties, so keep in mind that the energy from metals can drown out the energy of the crystals. Trust your intuition if you sense there is too much metal in one of your projects and see if you can adjust it so that the crystal isn't so covered in metal.

1

FOR

THE HOME

TERRARIUM GARDEN

DIFFICULTY ◆ ◇ ◇

A crystal-filled terrarium is a simple way to boost the
crystal power of a room, while also bringing some cute
plants into your home. Plants and crystals are both
formed from the earth, so they naturally complement
and support each other. This is a great way to bring
nature into your surroundings if you don't have a garden
or any outdoor space.

You will need

Glass terrarium or any large plant
*   holder: mine is approx. 22cm*
*   (8½in) high*
Fine gravel
Potting compost suitable for your chosen
*   plant*
Small succulent plants or cacti
Decorative gravel, polished pebbles,
*   stones or any other decorations*
Crystals of your choice

Crystal choice

For this project, I chose amethyst, one
of my favorite crystals. It is calming and
balancing and can have a strong protective
effect. I also added some quartz points,
which act to amplify the energy of the
amethyst. The quartz crystals are pointing
upwards to encourage an uplifting and
positive flow of energy in this garden.

STEP 1. Spend some time connecting to your reasons for picking the crystals you have chosen for this project. Work out your intention in creating your crystal garden. Is it to enhance the energy of your room? Is it to encourage your plant to grow? Is it to create a Zen garden and radiate those calm vibes in your home? Think about the answers to these questions when you come to lay the crystals out in a pattern or grid around your plants in step 5.

2

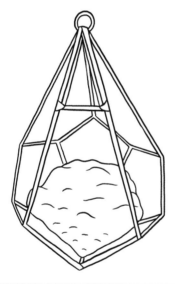

3

STEP 2. Place enough fine gravel in the terrarium to cover the base to a depth of at least 5mm (¼ in). On top of this, add approximately 5cm (2in) of compost. Make a well in the center where you wish your plants to sit.

STEP 3. Now plant your succulents or cacti in the compost and ensure they are firmly placed. Add more soil around the bases if needed. If your plants are particularly big or prickly, you may want to start by arranging the crystals and then add your plants after. (Be careful with the spines if you chose a cactus—you may need some gardening gloves!)

4

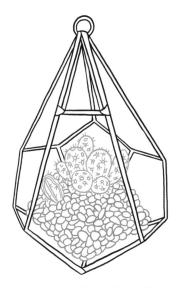

5

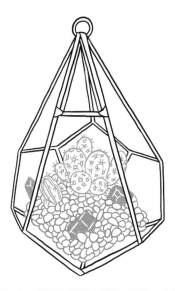

STEP 4. Add a layer of decorative gravel, polished pebbles or stones around your plants, gently pressing them into place to secure your plants and soil neatly. The stones will also help retain the moisture around your plant.

STEP 5. Consciously arrange your crystals in a grid, pattern or random design inside the terrarium. When you position the crystals, take note of how it looks and feels: does the pattern feel good when you look at it? Play around with your design until it feels right.

When your terrarium is complete, you can add another layer of magick: infuse the crystals with your intentions by talking to your plants and crystals regularly. Repeating loving words will affirm the energy in the plants and can really support them in staying strong and healthy!

ALTAR

An altar is a foundation for mindful daily practice and positive energy. You are dedicating a space in your home for your crystals to be seen and appreciated. A crystal altar can enhance and clear the energy of a room, and give you a focus for your crystal practice.

You will need

A cleansing item, e.g. a candle, palo santo, incense, sage
Sacred objects, e.g. tarot cards, a photo, a prayer, or written affirmation
Crystals, cleansed and set with intentions
Objects to represent the four elements (I used flowers for earth, a vase of water for water, a candle for fire, and a feather for air)

Crystal choice

Selenite is a must for me on my altar as it has such a pure and cleansing energy. I created this altar during a new moon with the intention of bringing daily reverence into my life. Ask yourself, which crystals feel good in your room and what do they amplify and support you with in your home and daily life?

Begin by choosing a space where the altar will be undisturbed and safe. It could be a corner of your room, a shelf, or an entire cabinet. Consider if the spot will get a lot of sunlight—over time, sunlight can fade colored stones. Cleanse this space.

Place the objects and crystals on your altar. You could do this in a mandala or a grid design, but do it intuitively, in a way that pleases you. It is important to include items connected with each of the four elements (earth, wind, water, and fire) to maintain the balance of your altar. Consider which objects are particularly meaningful to you: place these at the heart of your altar, beside the biggest crystals.

You might like to start a daily practice, such as lighting a candle on your altar and taking a moment to appreciate your space and set an intention for your day.

AFFIRMATION FRAME

DIFFICULTY ◆ ◆ ◆

This frame is a great way to give a visual reminder of an affirmation or intention that you want to remember. Devise your unique and personal affirmation, and choose three crystals that you feel correspond to the idea you are putting forward. For this project I chose the affirmation "I am joyful."

You will need

3 crystals of your choice

Piece of card or thin cork board, cut to the size of your frame

Glue gun

Felt-tip pens (optional)

Photo frame

Crystal choice

For this project, I chose a combination of three crystals that I felt would go well with the affirmation I wanted to attach to the frame: "I am joyful." Smoky quartz (bottom) is a gentle crystal that helps us to stay balanced and calm; carnelian (center) is a confidence-boosting crystal; and rose quartz is a reminder of love and compassion. As ever, trust your intuition as to which crystals are the right ones for your affirmation.

STEP 1. Take some deep breaths and connect with how you are feeling and what affirmation you would like to create. Choose crystals that you feel drawn to and make you feel connected to your affirmation. Ask yourself "what would I like to feel more of in my life?"

For me, it is joy, and my affirmation is: I AM JOYFUL. Perhaps for you, it is trust or confidence. Crystals help us connect to the energy we are sending out, so it will make all the difference to spend a few moments tuning in to the feeling you wish to amplify.

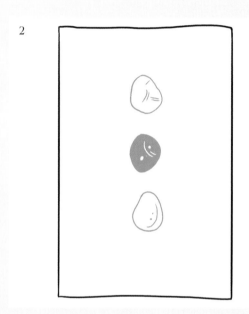

STEP 2. When you have your affirmation ready, hold the crystals to your heart and set your intention. In the example of an affirmation for joy, you could say, "I ask these crystals to bring more joy into my life." Every time you look at the affirmation frame, you will be reminded of your intention. When you are ready, arrange the crystals on the card.

STEP 3. Heat up your glue gun and glue each crystal on to the card with a small dot of glue. The great thing about a glue gun is that using it doesn't damage the crystals, so they can be reused if you want to change your affirmation. If you would like to write your affirmation on the card, you can do so now, or you can leave the frame with just the crystals. Do what feels best when it comes to reminding you of your intention.

STEP 4. Put the piece of card with the crystals in the frame (without the glass, as it won't fit with the crystals in place). Place your frame somewhere you will see it often, where it will remind you of your affirmation.

I

AM

JOYFUL!

CANDLE

DIFFICULTY ◆ ◆ ◇

Lighting a candle can feel like a sacred act: it can bring a deep sense of calm and wellbeing. These feelings are amplified by the crystals you choose to use in this project. You could choose to wait until a new moon or full moon and make it a ritual to light your candle. You could also infuse the crystals with a particular intention, so that when you burn the candle, that energy will radiate all around the room and into your life.

You will need

200ml (1 cup) water

Saucepan

225g (1 cup) soy wax flakes

Heatproof jug, to fit inside saucepan

Small metal whisk

2 tsp essential oil fragrance blend of
    your choice

Tea towel or oven glove

Heatproof glass candle jar, approx.
    275–300ml (1–1¼ cups)

Wooden wick

3 crystals of your choice

Dried petals, such as rose or calendula

Crystal choice

For this candle, I chose a combination of citrine and rose quartz crystals. I wanted to infuse the candle with clarity and loving energy. This is a good project to learn more about the innate energy of different crystals so that you can match the crystal to the effect you want to produce. You could try creating a candle for clarity using clear quartz, or a candle for creativity with amethyst, for example—but don't forget to use your intuition, too!

STEP 1. Heat the water in the saucepan over a low heat. Put all of the soy wax flakes into the jug and place the jug inside the saucepan. Be careful while melting the wax, as it can be flammable. Keep the heat low and stir the wax continuously with the whisk— it will eventually reach the right temperature and start to melt quite quickly. Once the wax has all melted, pour in the essential oils and give it a gentle whisk.

3

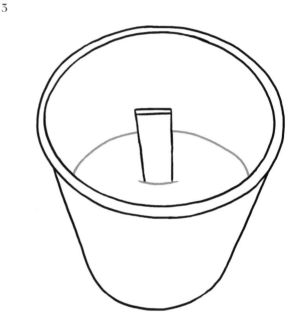

2

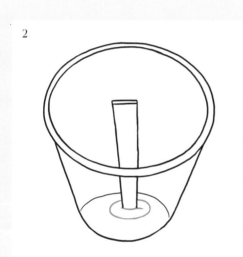

STEP 2. Take the pan and jug off the heat and lift the jug out of the hot water with an oven glove or tea towel. Carefully, pour a small circle of wax into the bottom of the candle jar. Place the wooden wick in the center of the candle jar and push it gently into the wax to hold it in place. Let this cool for a few minutes. You will see the wax change color as it sets.

STEP 3. If the wax in the jug has started to set, you can heat it up again using the pan of water. Once fully melted, pour about two thirds of what is left into the candle jar.

5

4

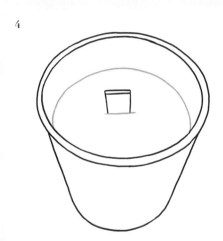

STEP 4. Leave the candle in a cool place to set—it should set quite quickly. Once this layer of wax has set, you can pour in the remainder of the wax (reheating as necessary).

STEP 5. As this final layer begins to set, but before it completely hardens, place your crystals and flower petals on top and gently press them into the wax. This may take some trial and error; if the wax isn't set enough, the crystals can sink below the surface of the candle. When you're happy with the decorations, leave the candle to set completely. Light the candle to feel the presence of the crystals and the intentions that you infused them with.

ARTWORK

DIFFICULTY ◆ ◆ ◆

This project uses crystals to amplify and express your innate creativity, and to make a beautiful piece of art for you to enjoy in your home. As you paint, remember that it's not about finding perfection: it's about going outside the lines, getting into your flow, and expressing yourself.

You will need
Cleansed crystals of your choice

Acrylic or watercolor paints in a selection of colors

Paintbrushes, large and small

Jar, water and cloth for washing brushes

Artist's canvas, or canvas board

Pencil

Chalk or other materials you would like to add

Glue gun

Crystal choice
You can either choose crystals that match your design, or create your design to work with your crystals! I chose a round rose quartz and quartz points and set them to amplify their natural energy of love, clarity, and creativity, which will shine wherever I place this painting.

STEP 1. Begin by setting your intention with your crystals. Try tuning in to their energy for inspiration for your artwork. Here, I have decided to paint a simple flower mandala design.

STEP 2. Next, mix up the color you would like for the background. Dilute this with some water and use a large brush to paint a wash all over your canvas. This gives you a foundation of color to build from.

STEP 3. Once the background is dry, you can start creating your design. Draw the outline in pencil first. Think about the placement of your crystals in this design, so you know where they will fit in the final piece. Once you're happy, you can begin to paint. Get as creative as you like: you could add neon colors, chalk, textures—whatever resonates with you in the moment. Art is a unique expression of your inner self—this is the beauty of handmade items. If you are painting a similar design to mine, I suggest starting from the central point.

STEP 4. Paint and fill in all the other aspects of your design, adding some lighter and darker shades to the edges to give more depth and dimension. For the little dots on this design, I used the end of a paintbrush dipped in white paint.

STEP 5. Wait for all the paint to dry. Then, heat up the glue gun, place a small dot of glue on each crystal, and push it into place on your artwork. Hang it somewhere you can appreciate and reflect on your creative expression. Don't forget to wash your paintbrushes afterwards!

It's not about perfection: it's about going outside of the lines, getting into your flow and expressing yourself

WINDOW CHARM

DIFFICULTY ◆ ◆ ◆

This crystal decoration is a great way to beam sparkles into your room when the sun shines. The project uses three crystals, but you can use as many as you like—you could even choose a crystal for each chakra (see page 20). This window charm would make a wonderful gift for someone who has just moved house!

You will need

6 x 30cm (12in) pieces of 0.5mm
   (24 gauge) silver wire
3 cleansed crystals of
   your choice
Pliers (round-nose,
   flat-nose, and cutters)
4 x 0.5mm silver jump rings
Keyring
Small piece of silver chain (optional)
Any other charms or
   beads you wish to add

Crystal choice

I chose fluorite crystals found in Cornwall, England for this project. They have beautiful tones of purple and green. Fluorite can help with grounding spiritual energy and supporting us emotionally. I love the feel of fluorite, and having it hanging in a room feels very soothing. Choose crystals you feel drawn to place in the room you are creating the window charm for; try quartz for positive and uplifting energy, or for socializing and creating, you could try carnelian.

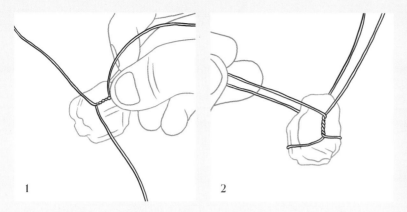

1

2

STEP 2. Wrap the bottom two wires around to the other side of the crystal (this will be the bottom part of the charm). Now secure them together with a few more twists. Try to line up the wires and keep them straight. You could also make patterns in the wire if you prefer a more organic look.

STEP 1. Take two pieces of wire, lay one across the other at the mid-point and make several twists to secure them together. Hold the twisted part against the center of your chosen crystal.

STEP 3. Repeat step 2 once or twice more, working up your crystal until you reach the top of it. Then make a few small twists on each side and join all of the wires together, twisting to secure the crystal fully.

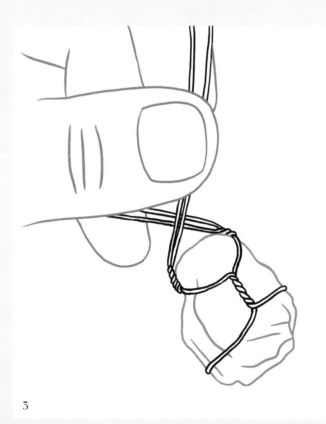

3

STEP 4. Separate the wires so that two are pointing upwards, then trim the other two and wind them around the top of the crystal, tucking the ends in neatly.

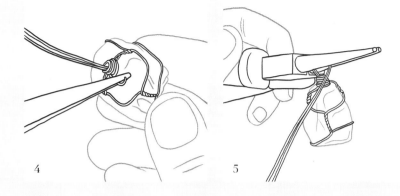

4

5

STEP 5. Next, wrap the remaining two wires around your round-nose pliers to form a neat loop. Hold the loop with the pliers and wrap the wire ends around the bottom of the loop a few times.

STEP 6. Trim the ends of the wires, bend them with the round-nose pliers and tuck them neatly under the loop.

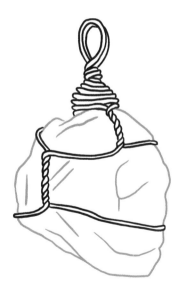

6

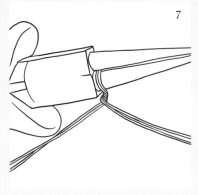

STEP 7. Now move on to the next crystal. Take another two wires, hold them together and find the mid-point. Make a fold in the wires here, wrap the middle around your round-nose pliers and twist the wires together a couple of times to secure the loop. This loop will form the bottom of the crystal wrap.

STEP 8. Separate the four wires and fit your crystal inside. Then bring the wires up the sides of the crystal, encasing it securely. Depending on the shape of the crystal, you may wish to make a twist in two of the wires halfway up to hold it in place.

STEP 9. Repeat steps 4, 5, and 6 on the previous page to finish the other end of the wire, wrapping it around to create a neat loop.

STEP 10. Repeat steps 7, 8, and 10
9 for the final crystal. Now you can
link the crystals with the jump rings.
Open the rings using the round-nose
and flat-nose pliers and then attach
the crystals, top to bottom, by their
loops, in any order and direction
you like. Close each of the rings
with the flat-nose pliers.

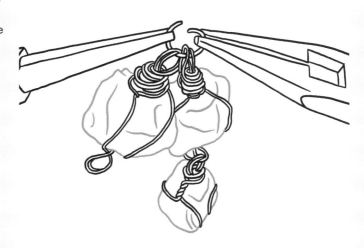

STEP 11. If you would like a short 11
hanger, you can attach the keyring
now; otherwise, you could add
a length of chain as well as any
charms or beads you wish to add.
Now you are ready to hang your
window charm!

Be mindful that certain
kinds of crystals can
fade if they are in
direct sunlight over
long periods of time.

MACRAMÉ PLANT HANGER

DIFFICULTY ◆ ◆ ◆

This macramé hanger is a great way to display a plant in your home. It saves space, as you can hang it from a curtain rail or hook, and the suspended crystal is able to radiate energy all around your room as well as supporting your plant's growth. Choose a plant pot and cord color to suit your chosen crystal and the décor of your home.

You will need

5cm (2in) hollow brass or wooden ring

15cm (6in) piece of string

6 x 4m (4½yd) pieces of 3mm (1/8in) cotton string (I used recycled cord)

15cm (6in) diameter plant pot

Crystal of your choice

Tape measure

30cm (12in) piece of 3mm (1/8) cotton cord (to finish off the design).

Scissors

Plant of your choice (I used a pelargonium)

Crystal choice

For this project, I chose rose quartz. Its beautiful pink hue really complements the natural green of the plant and the white of the string, and this crystal radiates loving energy. Choose a crystal you feel will work well hanging in your room and show some plant appreciation!

1

2

3

STEP 1. Start by securing the brass or wooden ring with the 15cm (6in) piece of string to something quite high up, such as a curtain rail. This will make your life easier as you start to knot the strings, and lead to fewer tangles. Make sure it is secure before you carry on.

STEP 2. Take one of the long strings and fold it in half. Pass the folded end through the ring and thread the loose ends through the loop this creates to secure the string.

STEP 3. Repeat step 2 with a second piece of string. You will now have four strings hanging down.

4

STEP 4. Now you are going to make a square knot. Separate the strings so you have two in the center, one on the left side, and one on the right side. Take the right-side string and fold it over the middle two, and grip it here with your left hand to make a backwards number 4 shape.

5

6

7

STEP 5. Keeping hold of the cords in your left hand, with your right hand, now cross the end of the left string over the right string, under the middle two strings and up through the loop created in step 4.

STEP 6. Pull the full length of the string through.

STEP 7. Pull this knot taut, up to the ring.

8

9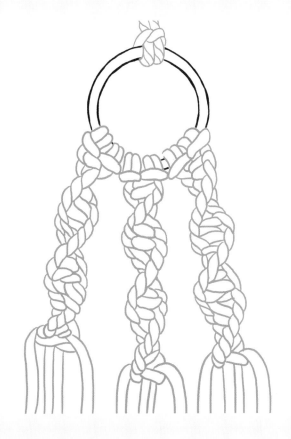

STEP 8. Repeat steps 4–7 for about 16 knots. The knots will create a twisting spiral pattern.

STEP 9. Now repeat steps 2–8 twice more on the same ring until you have three spiraling sections of knots.

 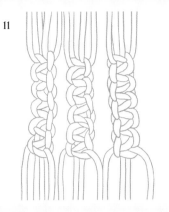

STEP 10. Make sure the strings hanging down from the knots are flat and not overlapping each other. Move down the strings to leave a 15cm (6in) gap before you begin to make some new knots. Start with the central set of four strings, and begin by creating one square knot as in steps 4–7. Instead of doing exactly the same knot below it, however, reverse the order so that this time you start with the left string. Alternate these knots for about ten knots and you will have a flat section of square knots.

STEP 11. Repeat step 10 for the other two sets of four strings.

STEP 12. Leave another gap and create a small section of five spiraling square knots (as in steps 4–7) in the central set. Repeat across all sets of strings.

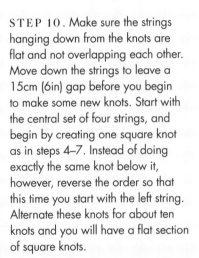

13

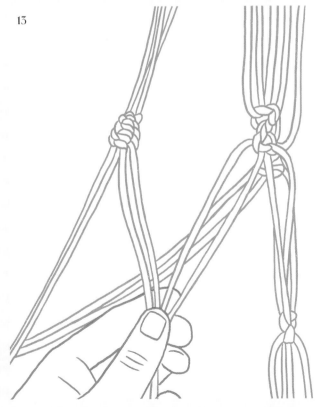

STEP 13. Now you are going to combine the three sets of strings to create a net for the plant pot. Leave a gap of about 7cm (2¾ in) from the last set of knots and take the left two strings from the central set and the right two strings from the left-hand set. Use these four strings to create three flat square knots (see step 10). Be sure to keep your strings in order!

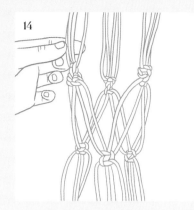

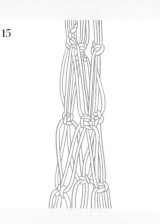

STEP 14. Repeat step 13, but use the right two strings of the central section and the left two strings of the right-hand section. Repeat once more with the remaining four strings so that all of the sections link up into three new sections of knots.

STEP 15. Leave another 7cm (2¾ in) gap and repeat steps 13 and 14, continuing the net.

STEP 16. Without leaving a gap this time, repeat steps 13–14 once more, pulling these knots together. This forms the bottom of the net for the plant pot.

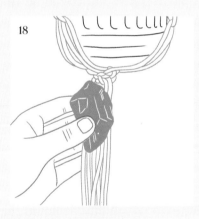

STEP 17. This is a good point to check that your pot fits nicely. If for any reason it doesn't fit, you can undo the last set of knots and make the space smaller or bigger by adjusting the gap between the sets of knots.

STEP 18. Take your crystal and hold it against the strings to get a sense of how much space to leave before your next set of knots.

STEP 19. Leaving the desired space, take four of the strings and make two square knots. Repeat this for the other two sets of four strings, as in step 14.

20

21

STEP 20. To finish off the design, hold all the strings together below the crystal. Take your 30cm (12in) piece of string in the same hand and fold the end over unevenly, so that one end hangs down by about 10cm (4in). The top of the loop should sit just beneath the last knots.

STEP 21. Take the long end of the string and wrap it around the strings, moving upwards. Try to keep this as tight and neat as you can.

STEP 22. Once you get to the top, pass the end through the loop and pull gently on the other end at the bottom of the wrapping. This will pull the string down so you can't see the loose top end. Trim the end of the wrapping string and trim the ends of all the long strings dangling down as short or long as you would like. Your plant is now ready to hang up in your home.

22

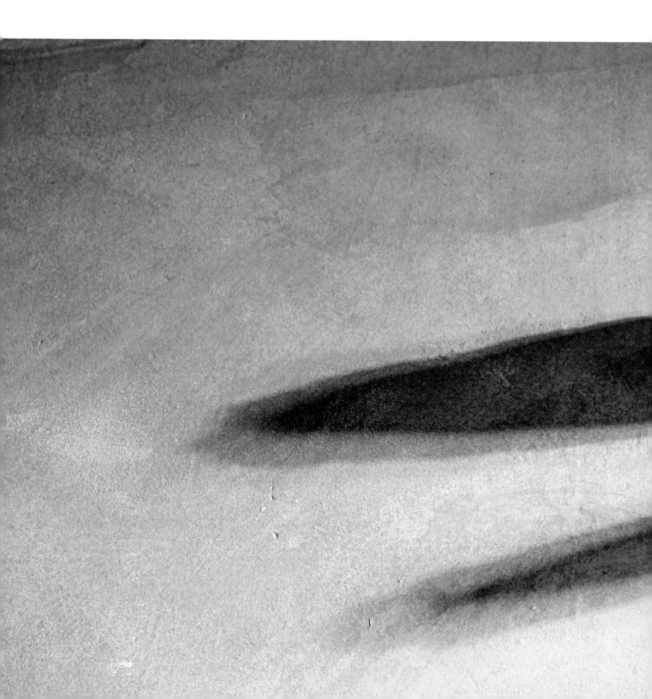

TO WEAR

HAIRPIN

This hairpin is a chic way to add a crystal to your hair, and to keep crystals close to your mind all day. You could create a whole set of hairpins with different crystals, and choose the one with the right energy for whatever your day has in store.

You will need

2 x 20cm (8in) pieces of 0.5mm
    (24 gauge) copper wire
Small crystal of your choice (choose
    a good shape to wire wrap)
6cm (2¼in) bobby pin
Pliers (round-nose, flat-nose, and cutters)

Crystal choice

I chose a quartz for this hairpin because the clear energy of this crystal can be great for clarifying the mind and helping you feel uplifted. It's the perfect crystal to wear on your head!

1

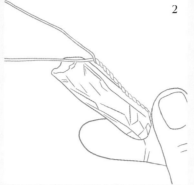

2

3

STEP 1. Lay one wire across the other at the mid-point and twist them together several times.

STEP 2. Keep twisting the two wires together until the twisted section is approximately three-quarters of the length of your crystal.

STEP 3. Place the twisted section along the edge of the crystal, and wrap two of the loose ends around the end of the crystal.

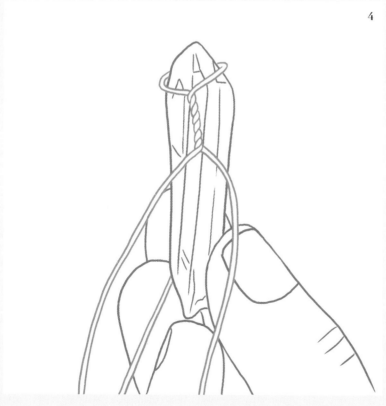

4

STEP 4. Create a similar twisted section on the opposite side of the crystal, making sure to enclose the crystal securely. Keep on twisting until it is the same length as the twisted section on the first side.

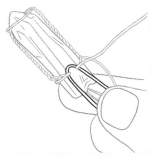 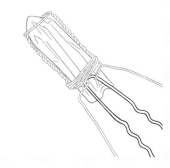

STEP 5. Now place the bobby pin at what will be the back of the crystal and wrap each wire underneath each prong of the hairpin.

STEP 6. Align the hairpin to where you would like it to sit and then, one wire at a time, begin wrapping the excess wire around the crystal, just covering the top of the hairpin.

STEP 7. Once you have wrapped the wire around enough times, you can trim the end, bend it, and tuck it behind the wrapped wire so that it is hidden and no sharp edges stick out.

Repeat this with all of the wires until you are happy the crystal is secure and the wires look neat (or messy, depending on your style!).

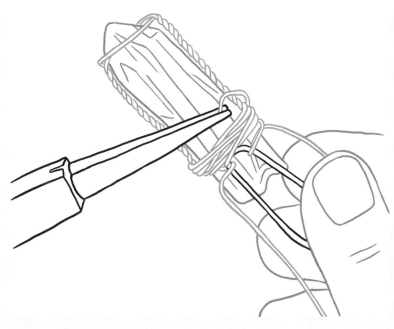

EARRINGS

Wearing crystals adds their energy to your aura. If there is a certain type of energy you would like to bring into your life, then wearing the corresponding crystal can support you with this. If you decide to make these earrings as a gift for a friend, think about what sort of crystal energy would benefit them and choose the crystals accordingly.

You will need
Selection of crystal and glass beads
(I used quartz and natural citrine
chip beads combined with yellow
4mm (1/8in) faceted glass beads
for extra sparkle)
2 x 15cm (6in) pieces of 0.4mm
(26 gauge) silver-plated wire
(or other color of your choice)
Pliers (round-nose, flat-nose, and cutters)
2 x 0.5mm silver jump rings
2 hypoallergenic wire earring hooks in
your choice of color

Crystal choice
For these earrings, I chose to pair citrine and quartz. Citrine is a crystal that radiates joyful energy and creativity, and combining it with quartz amplifies these qualities. If this project is for a gift, you could also think about the recipient's favorite colors, or which crystals would complement their eyes or skin tone. Set an intention with your crystals before crafting with them—or wearing them—to connect more personally with their essence.

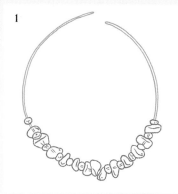

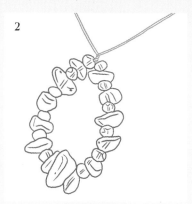

STEP 1. Slide a selection of your glass and crystal beads on to the center of one of your pieces of silver-plated wire. Think about the order and design of the beads: which one would you like to hang at the center; how do you want to arrange the varying sizes of crystal?

STEP 2. Once you're happy with the design, twist the two ends of the wire together a couple of times close to the top of your beads to secure them in place.

STEP 3. Cut one end of the wire close to the twists you have just made, then gently twist and squeeze this loose end so that it sits against the twists as neatly as possible.

STEP 4. Take your round-nose pliers and wrap the other wire around one side of them once to make a loop. Make sure this loop is big enough for you to fit the jump ring through it.

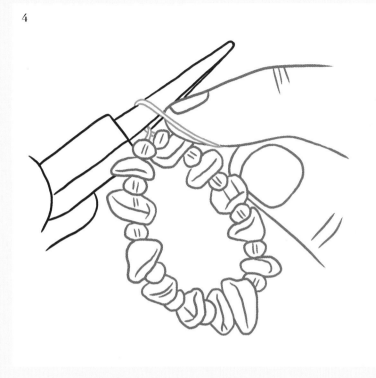

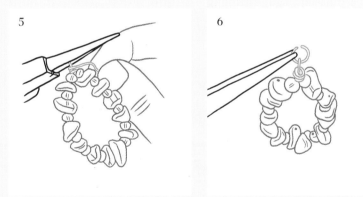

STEP 5. Hold the earring with the pliers and wrap the end of the wire underneath the loop a few times to cover the twists and add strength.

STEP 6. Using the round-nose and flat-nose pliers, open the jump ring and attach the earring and ear hook to it. Once they are attached, carefully squeeze the jump ring closed and make sure it is secure.

STEP 7. Repeat steps 1–6 to make the second earring.

RING

A crystal ring is a simple and subtle way to wear crystals, and they will be closely connected to the powerful chakras in your hands. You can also set an intention with your crystal ring for the day: when you put it on, take a moment to tune in to what you would like the crystal to support you with during the day ahead. It could be anything from gaining confidence for a meeting to feeling empathy for a challenging person in your life.

You will need
30cm (12in) piece of 0.8mm
   (20 gauge) silver-plated wire
Selection of crystal chip beads
Pliers (flat-nose, round-nose, and cutters)

Crystal choice
For this ring, I used rose quartz beads. The energy of rose quartz is very nurturing, and it is a reminder to stay connected to the power within and trust our hearts. You could use citrine for a confidence-boosting ring—or any crystal you feel drawn to.

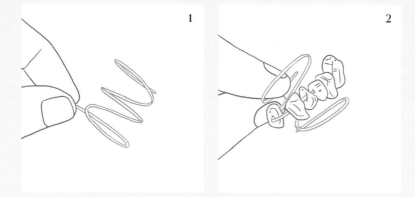

STEP 1. Wrap your wire three times around the finger you will wear the ring on to get a rough idea of size. Pull the wire spiral apart slightly so you have some space between each loop.

STEP 2. Thread a selection of crystal beads on to the wire to fill the central loop of your spiral. Take this opportunity to check that the ring has kept the shape needed to fit your finger.

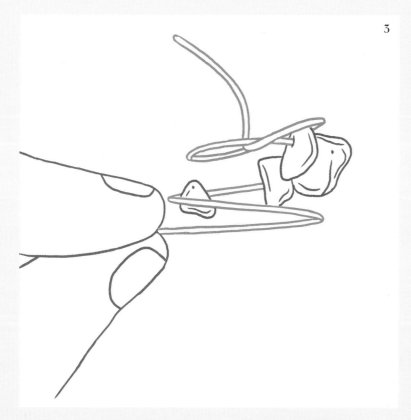

STEP 3. Take one of the ends of wire and wrap it around the central loop, where the beads finish on one side. Make a couple of twists and then cut the end.

STEP 4. Using the
flat-nose pliers, make
sure the end of the wire
is securely tucked away
so there are no sharp
edges poking out.

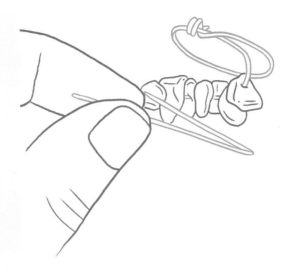

5

STEP 5. Check one
more time that the ring
still fits and then repeat
steps 3 and 4 with the
other end of the wire.
Make any final crimps
with the ends to secure
them neatly. Your new
crystal ring is now ready
to wear.

CROWN

Feel like a goddess with your own crystal crown. This crown feels glorious to wear for a creative meditation, some self-love indulgence or to express your creative crystal skills at a festival! Wire wrapping takes a lot of patience and practice to get the finished result you would like, but it is worth it for this lovely piece.

You will need

Cleansed crystals

Shells of your choice (optional)

Metal headband

Glue gun (optional)

5 x 1.5m (1¾yd) lengths of 0.5mm (24 gauge) silver or copper wire (if you have very large crystals and shells, you may need more pieces of wire)

Pliers (round-nose, flat-nose, and cutters)

Crystal Choice

I chose a spiral seashell for the centerpiece of this crown because the beach is one of my favorite places to be and shells really connect me to serene ocean vibes. I added four quartz points for an energizing and uplifting feeling. Quartz can store and raise positive energy, which can have an effect not only on you but also on the energy of those around you. A good headpiece to wear at parties!

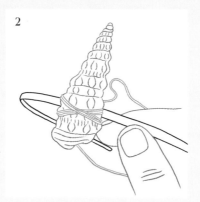

STEP 1. Arrange the crystals as you would like to position them on the headband. You could glue each one to the band with the glue gun to help keep them in place while you start wire wrapping. I find the glue usually comes off quite quickly, but it can help with this first step.

STEP 2. Holding the centerpiece crystal or shell in place, take a piece of wire, find roughly its middle, and wrap the wire around the piece and the headband. Make three diagonal wraps in one direction, then three in the opposite direction, so that it forms a cross pattern.

STEP 3. Now wrap one loose end of the wire around the metal headband in one direction, until you reach the spot on the headband where the next crystal will sit.

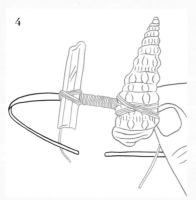

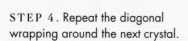

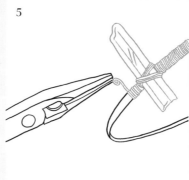

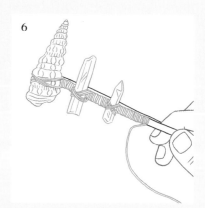

STEP 4. Repeat the diagonal wrapping around the next crystal.

STEP 5. To start a new piece of wire, fold it over the headband, leaving around 5cm (2in) at one end. Wrap this around the band a couple of times, then trim and make a tiny loop at the end of the wire. Fold this down to meet the end of the last wire.

STEP 6. Continue wrapping the wire and adding crystals until you are happy with the design. If a crystal is loose or the wire didn't wrap well, just undo the piece and add a new section of wire. Make sure you trim any sharp ends before wearing your crown!

PENDANT

DIFFICULTY ◆ ◆ ◆

The most traditional way to wear a crystal—the pendant necklace—is still a popular choice for crystal jewelry. You could hang the pendant on a chain or a simple string necklace, and the stone you choose will hang close to your heart all day. Alternatively, you could use this technique to hang crystals in any room to which you wish to add some positive energy.

You will need
2 x 80cm (32in) pieces of 0.5mm
    (24 gauge) silver-plated wire
A crystal of your choice (one with a long
    point will work best)
Pliers (round-nose, flat-nose, and cutters)
Necklace chain or piece of string/
    ribbon to thread the pendant on to

Crystal choice
For this project, I chose a piece of quartz with a single point. This crystal is a powerful energizer: it can bring a sense of power and help protect against negativity.

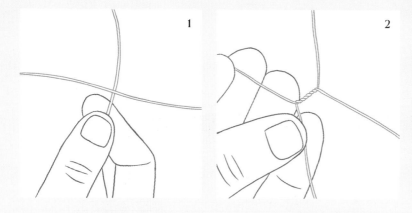

STEP 1. Take the two pieces of wire and bend each one lightly in the middle as a reference mid-point.

STEP 2. Cross the pieces of wire over at the mid-point and hold them securely in one hand while tightly twisting them together with your other hand. It may take some practice to get them to wrap tightly and neatly. Wrap the two wires together for about six twists.

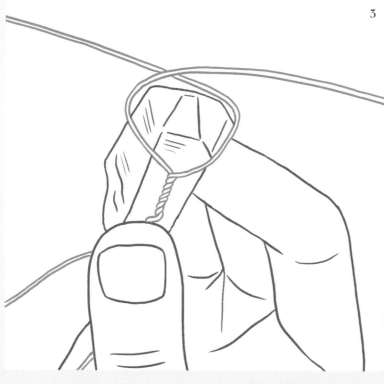

STEP 3. The two wires will now be attached with four free ends. Place the twisted part of the wire against the side of your crystal, close to the tip. Wrap the two wires nearest the tip around your crystal.

STEP 4. Twist the two wires together tightly on the other side of the crystal about six times. This step will create the bottom of the "cage" for your crystal to sit inside. Depending on the size and shape of your crystal, you will need to wrap and bend the wire to fit nicely against the side of the stone.

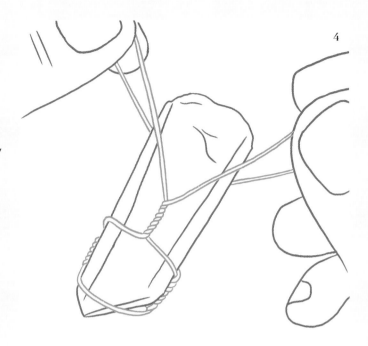

STEP 5. Take one wire from each twisted pair and bring these together along the side of the crystal. Twist together tightly about six times, and repeat with the two wires left on the other side of the crystal. Repeat this pattern all the way up the crystal. Use the flat-nose pliers to help shape the wire as you go along. Once you have reached almost to the top of the pendant, twist all four wires together and make a couple of final twists to secure the crystal.

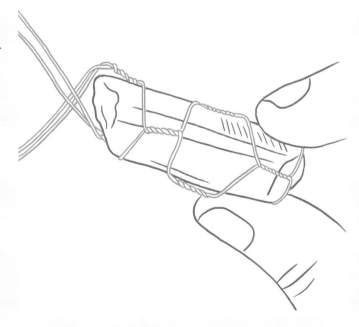

STEP 6. Trim two of the wires at the back of the pendant and tuck in using the round-nose pliers. Wrap the remaining two wires around the handle of your pliers, or any other thin, cylindrical object. Bring the ends around to the front to form the loop—you can adjust the shape with pliers or your fingers afterwards.

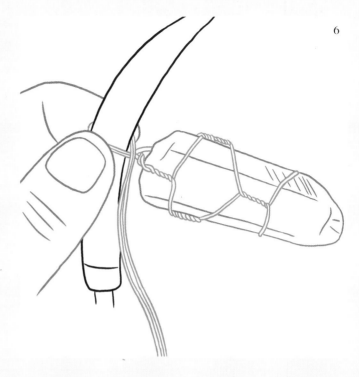

6

STEP 7. To finish the loop, wrap the remaining wires around the bottom of the loop, one at a time. Once you are happy with the wrapping, trim and bend the end of the wires underneath the loop to keep it neat and secure. Use your pliers to shape the bottom of the loop and compress everything to stop any of the wires from unraveling. You can then thread it on to a necklace chain or a piece of string/ribbon.

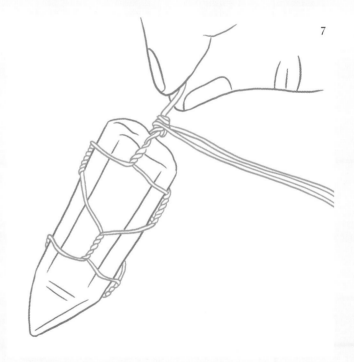

ANKLET

You can choose to wear this simple macramé piece as an anklet or a bracelet, as it is both pretty and strong. Wearing a crystal on your ankle or wrist can help crystal energy flow through you throughout the day, nourishing you with crystallized intent.

You will need

1m (40in) 0.5mm waxed polyester
    thread (such as Linhasita) or
    hemp cord
2.75m (3yd) 0.5mm waxed polyester
    thread (such as Linhasita) or
    hemp cord
Paintbrush or thin pencil
Cleansed crystal beads (I chose
    3mm (1/8in) hematite beads)
Scissors
Lighter/matches

Crystal Choice

I chose hematite for this project to create a grounding anklet. Hematite can help us feel connected to our roots and stabilize our foundations. This is a crystal I love to wear to keep me feeling balanced.

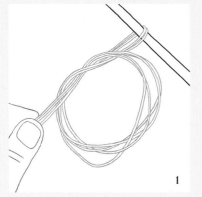 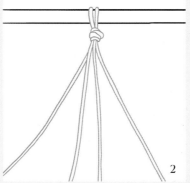 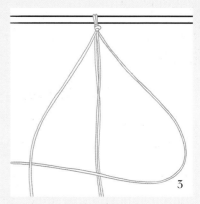

STEP 1. Take the two pieces of string and fold them both in half. Loop the center of both pieces around a thin pencil or paintbrush to get a neat loop—this will be the fastening for the end of the bracelet. Tie one overhand knot with both the strings beneath the loop.

STEP 2. Now you have four strings hanging from the knot. The two shorter strings will be the inner strings, and the two longer ones are the outer, working strings. It might be useful now to secure the paintbrush or pencil to something to make the next steps easier.

STEP 3. Fold the right working string over the inner strings to make a backwards number 4 shape.

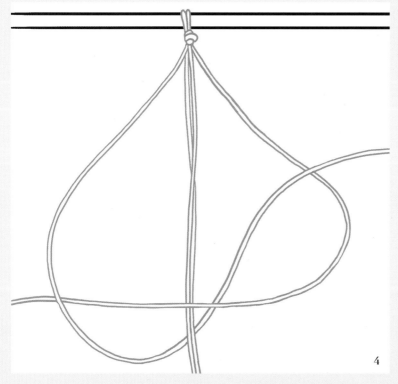

STEP 4. Now take the left working string and weave this over the right working string, underneath the inner strings, and through the loop made with the right string.

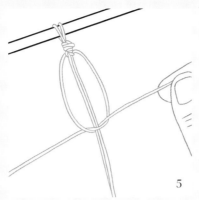

5

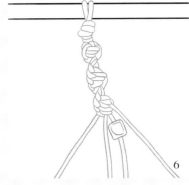

6

STEP 5. Pull the left and right working strings taut while keeping the inner strings straight.

STEP 6. Repeat steps 3–5 for about 2.5cm (1in) to begin your spiral pattern. Thread a crystal on to one of the inner strings, and continue knotting around it.

STEP 7. Keep knotting and adding beads at regular intervals. Once the anklet is the length you would like (try it around your ankle, or wrist if it's a bracelet, to make sure), tie all of the strings together at the end of the knots. Separate the loose strings into two sections, leave about 5cm (2in) of length and make a knot in each section. Trim the excess string after the knots and melt the ends carefully over a flame to give a neat finish. Slide the anklet off your paintbrush/pencil, and the loop you made to hang it by now becomes the loop to fasten it with.

7

TALISMAN

DIFFICULTY ◆ ◆ ◆

A talisman is an object that is infused with magick:
therefore, it creates favorable energy. Take your time
choosing a crystal that you feel drawn to wear. As you
craft your talisman, keep in mind that you are already
creating a connection with the crystal and infusing it with
your intention and energy.

You will need

3 x 120cm (48in) pieces of 0.5mm
    waxed polyester thread (such
    as Linhasita)

Small round pen or paintbrush

Cleansed crystal, approx. 3 x 4cm
    (1¼ x 1½in)

Any extra beads or charms you wish to
    add (optional)

Scissors

Lighter/matches

3 x 90cm (36in) pieces of 0.5mm
    waxed polyester thread (such
    as Linhasita)

Tape measure

Crystal choice

For this project, I chose a piece of natural
quartz that my sister found while hiking
in Cornwall, England. I love the natural,
organic shape of this crystal and I added
some glowing labradorite beads at the
bottom. Labradorite is a crystal that helps
bring out the magick within us and can
help us during times of change.

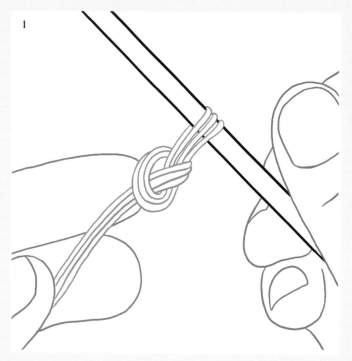

STEP 1. First, take the longer strings to create the pendant "cage." Fold the three strings in half and place them around the pen or paintbrush to make a neat loop. Now make one overhand knot below the loop with all six strands, and pull this knot nice and tight. Pull each string individually to make it secure.

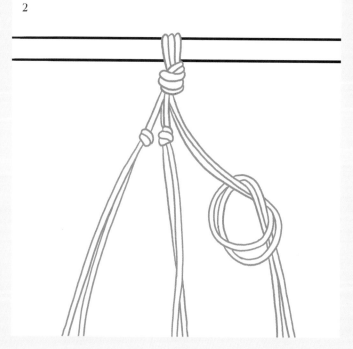

STEP 2. Separate the six strings into three groups of two. Hold two strings together and make one overhand knot with both strings, around 1cm (½in) from the top knot. Repeat this for the other two sets of strings.

STEP 3. Place your crystal inside the first row of knots and see how it fits. This is the top of your pendant. You need to work with the shape of the crystal you have chosen. Do not copy mine exactly; work with the unique dimensions of your own crystal.

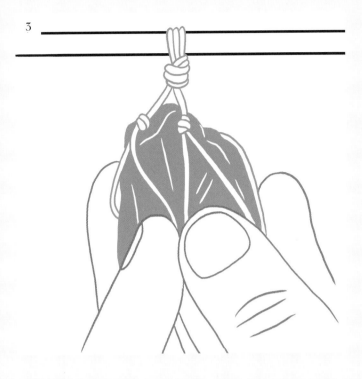

STEP 4. Take a string dangling from one knot and hold it together with a string from the neighboring knot. Make one overhand knot with these two strings that sits between and below the knots above.

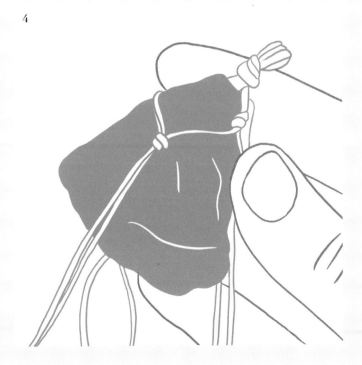

STEP 5. Continue as in step 4, around and down the crystal; this will start to create diamond shapes. Make sure you are leaving space for your crystal inside. You could tie the knots but not pull them too tight initially, waiting until you are sure they are in the right place.

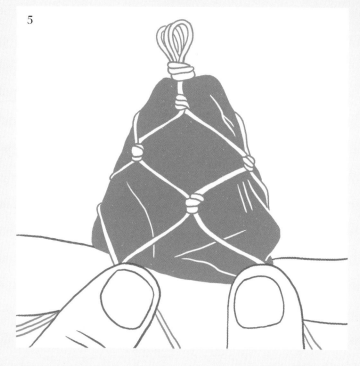

STEP 6. Once you get to the bottom of the talisman, hold all six strings together and make one overhand knot. Pull each string individually to secure the knot. You can add beads to the ends of the strings if you like; otherwise, simply cut the strings as close to the knot as you wish. Melt the ends carefully over a flame to give a neat finish.

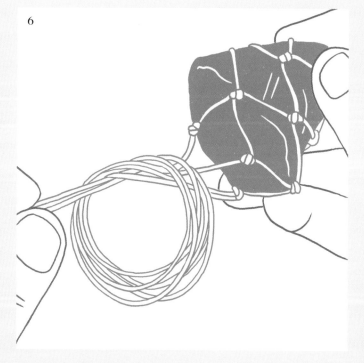

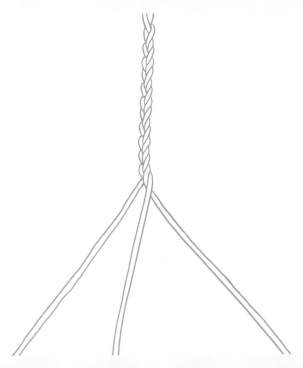

STEP 7. It is now time to make the necklace. Take the three remaining strings, tie them together with one overhand knot at the end, and secure to a board. Braid the three strings together all the way to the end. Tie another overhand knot to keep the braiding in place.

8

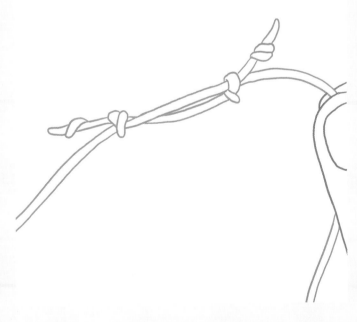

STEP 8. Thread your pendant on to the necklace. Make two sliding knots so that you can adjust the length of the talisman. Hold one end of the braided string over the top of the other end. Take the top string behind the bottom one and wrap it back around to the front. Now thread the end through the loop you have made, pull the end through, and tighten so the knot can still slide freely along the other string. Repeat this for the other string so you have two knots that slide. Trim and melt the ends of the strings.

3 FOR THE

BATHROOM

INFUSED
ESSENTIAL OILS

DIFFICULTY ◆ ◆ ◆

This handy roller bottle is something you can carry around with you and use whenever you need to feel refreshed and uplifted. Choose high-quality essential oils and seek guidance if you are unsure which to choose. You can apply essential oils to acupressure points, such as your wrists, temples, or the soles of your feet.

You will need

Small crystals or crystal beads

Glass roller-ball bottle (30ml/1oz size)

20ml (4 tsp) fractionated coconut oil, or other carrier oil

20 drops of essential oils (make sure they are safe to use on your skin and patch-test for any allergic reaction)

Flower petals

Crystal choice

For this blend, I chose to combine my favorite fragrances—frankincense and lavender—with amethyst crystals to infuse the oils with calm and peaceful energy. For a more energizing combination, you could try a citrus oil such as bergamot or orange, with bright crystals such as citrine or quartz.

Begin by holding your crystals to your heart to cultivate a deeper connection with them. Ask them to connect with you and infuse your daily life with the energy you need: it could be calmness or confidence, for example. Fill your roller-ball bottle with the coconut oil, then add the drops of your chosen essential oils. Add flower petals, then drop in your chosen crystals. Put the roller top back on the bottle: your essential oils are ready to go in your bag or your pocket for on-the-go crystal energy!

FACE MASK

DIFFICULTY ◆ ◆ ◆

Crystals can give us an energetic glow, and this face mask also utilizes the cleansing properties of kaolin clay and the brightening glow of turmeric to give you clear, bright skin. Kaolin clay is great for detoxifying skin, helping to gently remove impurities and reduce oiliness. The best part is, it's 100% natural! Always do a small patch-test to make sure your skin is happy with all of these ingredients before trying this mask out. You could also try other ingredients, like rose water or green tea, which are packed with enriching antioxidants.

You will need

3 tbsp kaolin clay powder

½ tsp turmeric

Glass or ceramic mixing bowl

1 tsp unrefined organic coconut oil

½ tsp honey (optional)

Wooden spoon (metal spoons can cause a reaction with the properties of the clay)

3 tbsp filtered water (enough to make a paste)

1 cleansed citrine crystal

Glass jar with lid (if you plan to store for later use)

Crystal choice

Citrine is a sunshine crystal that can brighten your mood and bring joyful frequencies into your life—perfect for this golden face mask to infuse your skin with a crystal glow!

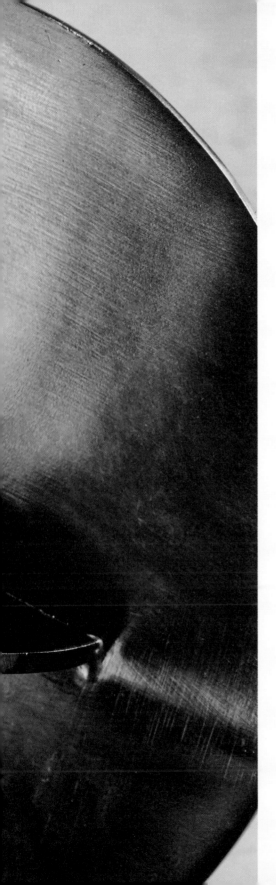

STEP 1. Combine the clay and turmeric in a bowl. Gently melt the coconut oil (and honey if you are using it) and pour it into the powder. Use a wooden spoon to mix well. Be careful with the turmeric as it can stain light-colored fabrics, as well as your hands if you don't wash it off thoroughly.

STEP 2. Slowly add the filtered water. The aim is to make a thick, paste-like consistency; if it is too liquid, it won't stick to your skin as well. Keep mixing until it is nice and smooth.

STEP 3. Once it is all mixed together, it is time to add the magick ingredient—your crystal. Hold the crystal in your hand and infuse it with your intention. It could be to look radiant or to feel happy from the inside out. Whatever resonates with you—that's the most important thing. Now place the crystal in the face mask mixture. Leave it in there for half an hour, or even overnight, if you have time.

STEP 4. Apply your face mask, carefully avoiding your mouth and eyes. Take 10–15 minutes to lie down, relax, and let the minerals invigorate your skin. You could also put the crystal on your forehead to feel the crystal energy while the face mask works its magick! Listen to some soothing sounds and allow yourself this time to recharge.

STEP 5. With a washcloth and some warm water, rinse off thoroughly and say hello to your radiant, fresh face! If you would like to keep this face mask a little longer, store it in a glass jar in the fridge. Use it within a week for best results—the fresher, the better.

SELF-CARE
BATH POTION

DIFFICULTY ◆ ◆ ◆

Make a date with your bathtub to relax and indulge your senses. Epsom salts are great for relieving muscle tension and detoxing the body, and the addition of flowers and herbs, plus your crystal, can really elevate a bath.

You will need

Mixing bowl

Epsom salts (enough to almost fill your container)

Your choice of flowers or herbs (e.g. rose petals, lavender, sage, and calendula)

Crystal of your choice

Glass bottle or jar with a cork or lid

In a bowl, mix the Epsom salts with your flowers and herbs of choice. Hold your crystal to your heart and take a deep breath. Infuse the crystal with your intention and connect to its energy. What would you like to feel when you bathe? You could ask the crystal to support you with cleansing, relaxing, and appreciating everything your body does for you.

Crystal choice

I usually choose rose quartz to infuse my bathwater with loving and healing energy. After a long week of work or a particularly emotional day, rose quartz is a wonderful crystal to help relax, balance, and restore energy, with a particular focus on the heart. Remember to only choose crystals that are suitable for immersion.

Place the crystal in the jar, then pour in your bath potion blend. It will keep for a long time in this way if it is kept dry. You can also try putting your crystal directly into your bathwater, then sprinkling in a handful of your bath potion

4 GIFTS

& TRINKETS

INFUSED WATER

DIFFICULTY ◆ ◆ ◆

Adding crystals to water is thought by some to help to purify and add certain energies to the water. Shungite can be a good crystal to start adding to your water, as it is commonly used in water filters. Take breaks from drinking this water to give your body a chance to adjust and yourself a chance to notice any differences you experience, as well as whether you are sensitive to its effects.

You will need

Cleansed and sterilized crystal

Water storage bottle or jug (preferably glass or stainless steel)

Stainless steel tea infuser (optional)

Crystal choice

I used shungite crystals, but you could experiment with various crystals: rose quartz for peaceful, loving vibes; amethyst for calming energy; citrine for clarity and trust. Remember there are certain crystals that shouldn't be stored in water or used for infusion, so always check this first.

Set your intention with your chosen crystal by holding it close to your heart. Your intention could be something like, "I ask this crystal to purify this water and fill it with light." If you like visual techniques, you could visualize the water being filled with a golden, crystalline light.

You can also speak an affirmation into your water; just like crystals, water can hold energy and vibrational imprints. Once you feel the crystal has received your intention or affirmation, place it into a jug or bottle of water. If you like, you can put it in a tea infuser, for easy removal.

KEYRING

Keys are something we usually have with us all the time, and they often carry associations with certain places, like home or work, so a keyring is a great way to keep your crystals with you. Crystals can amplify our ability to manifest certain situations and feelings. What do you need in your daily life to help you feel more flow?

You will need

30cm (12in) piece of 0.5mm (24 gauge) silver wire

1 small silver charm

Approx. 8 crystal chip beads of your choice (I also included two rose colored beads from an old necklace I upcycled)

Pliers (round-nose, flat-nose, and cutters)

1 x 0.5mm silver jump ring

Silver keyring clasp

Crystal choice

I love the combination of clear quartz and rose quartz with these pearlescent beads. I chose rose quartz because it's a reminder to stay in contact with our hearts throughout the day. You could use any crystal that you feel you need to take on your travels through daily life or to help you in a certain aspect of it. Clear quartz has a clarifying energy, which can support living our lives with balance, calm, and perspective.

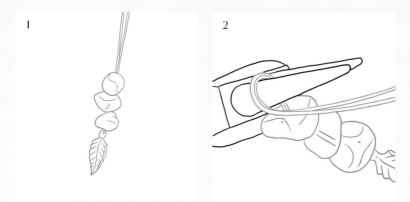

STEP 1. Fold the piece of wire in half. Thread the silver charm on to one end of the wire and slide it down so that it sits at the fold in the wire. Thread both ends of wire through your chosen beads and crystals in your desired pattern.

STEP 2. Once you are happy with your design, take the round-nose pliers and hold the wires in the middle of them, just above the crystals and beads. Now wrap the wires up and around the pliers to create a loop.

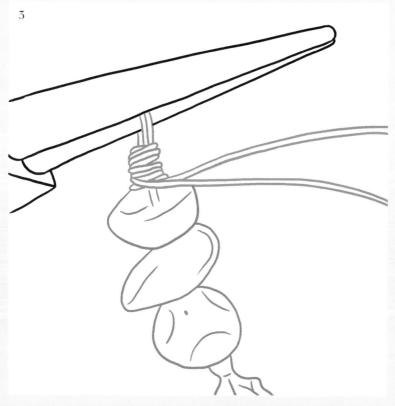

STEP 3. Twist the two wires around and wrap them a few times underneath the loop to neaten it. This is good practice for creating wire loops and wire wrapping, which will help with a lot of the other projects in this book!

4

STEP 4. Cut one of the wires, bend the end, and neatly tuck it underneath the loop. Now wrap the remaining wire around once more, then trim and tuck it away in the same way. Use the flat-nose pliers to give it a crimp close.

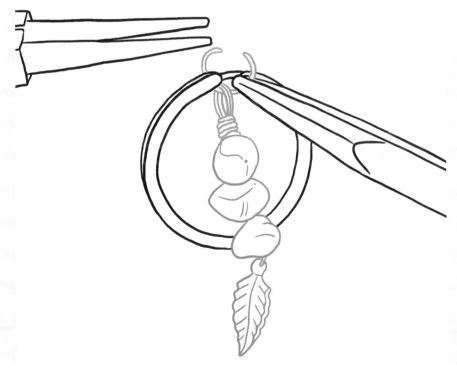

5

STEP 5. Using the round-nose and flat-nose pliers, open the jump ring. Thread on the wire loop and the keyring clasp and press the jump ring closed with the flat-nose pliers.

DRAWSTRING POUCH

DIFFICULTY ◆ ◆ ◆

A friend of mine started making little upcycled bags, and as soon as I saw them, I immediately thought they would be perfect for keeping crystals safe on the go! Carry them in your pocket with you, or use them as sweet crystal gift bags for friends and family. I won't be winning any awards for my sewing skills, but this cute pouch is really simple to make even if you're totally new to sewing.

You will need

Piece of fabric measuring 23 x 11.5cm (9 x 4½in)—I used some pre-loved floral cloth

25cm (10in) piece of cotton cord

Pen/pencil

Needle

Thread

Scissors

Safety pin

Cleansed crystal(s) to put in your pouch

Crystal choice

You can keep any crystals you like in this cute drawstring pouch. I like to ask myself which crystals or energy I feel I need for the day ahead. One day I may feel drawn to a piece of smoky quartz for emotional balance, or another day the sunny glow of citrine will stand out to me.

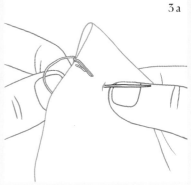

STEP 1. Fold your rectangular piece of fabric in half, right sides together (inside out), to make a square shape.

STEP 2. The fold will be the bottom of your bag. Place your cord close to the top, fold a little of the fabric over and adjust so that the cord has enough space to move. Mark the line you're going to sew along and remove the cord.

STEP 3. Sew along your marked line using running stitch to create the drawstring channel. Secure the thread at each end with a few tiny overlapping stitches. Repeat steps 2 and 3 to make the channel for the other side of the pouch.

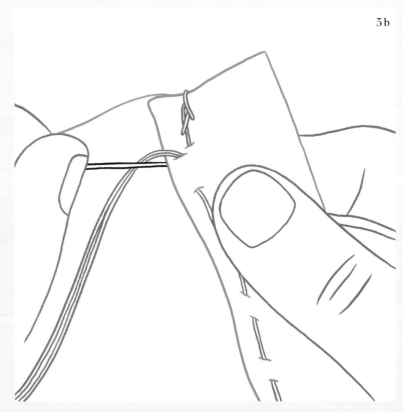

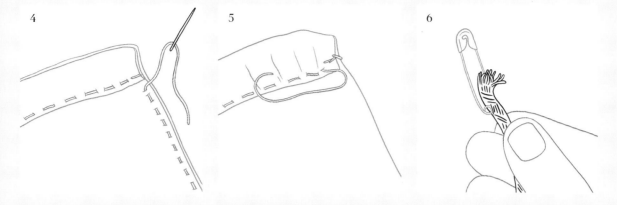

STEP 4. Now sew together the sides of the pouch using running stitch until you meet the drawstring channel stitching. Make sure your stitches are close enough together so that, if you place a tiny crystal in the bag, it won't slip out.

STEP 5. Use a couple of small stitches to sew the two drawstring sections together at one end of the pouch, so that they are joined together, but leave the other end open for the string to pass through.

STEP 6. Attach one end of the cord to the safety pin. Use the safety pin to help you thread the cord into its drawstring channel, wiggling it through the openings you left for it. Once the cord has come out at the other end, tie an overhand knot in each end of the cord. Finally, turn your bag inside out to reveal the finished product.

BOOKMARK

I love picking up a book when I am traveling or after finishing a day of work. Reading is exercise for the brain, and allows us to immerse ourselves in other worlds and absorb knowledge. Adding a crystal bookmark to your reading ritual can boost the clarity you feel when reading your favorite book, or while taking in new information.

You will need

Selection of crystal beads of your choice

2 x 13mm (½in) ribbon clasps

22cm (8½in) length of 13mm (½in) ribbon of your choice (could be shorter or longer, depending on your book size)

Pliers (flat-nose, round-nose, and cutters)

2 x 30cm (12in) pieces of 0.5mm (24 gauge) silver wire

2 x 0.5mm silver jump rings

Crystal choice

For this bookmark, I chose clear quartz to help me focus on what I am reading. I often read books about philosophy, and when my mind feels clear, I find I can absorb much more of the information. Quartz can also be great for sparking your imagination when reading fiction.

all day on the roof waiting for him

STEP 1. Choose the crystal combination you would like and focus your intention with the crystals by holding them to your heart and charging them with your thoughts.

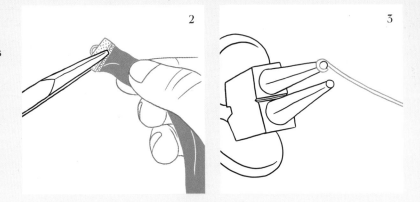

STEP 2. Take one of the ribbon clasps and put one end of the ribbon inside it. Using the flat-nose pliers, squeeze the clasp closed firmly on both sides. Repeat this with the other ribbon clasp on the other end of the ribbon.

STEP 3. Wrap the end of one of the wires around the narrow end of one of the round-nose pliers to create the start of a spiral.

STEP 4. With the flat-nose pliers, crimp the end in tightly and curl the wire round on itself to create a spiral. Keep doing this until you have a small, flat spiral.

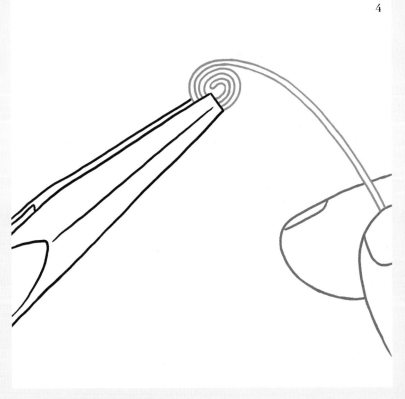

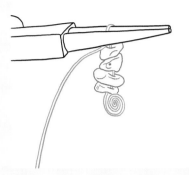

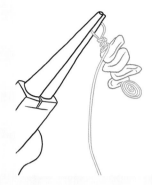

6

STEP 5. Thread your chosen crystal beads on to your wire so they sit above the spiral. Then wrap the wire around the round-nose pliers to create a loop just above the crystal beads.

STEP 6. Twist the long end of the wire around the base of the loop several times and trim off the excess. Bend and tuck in the end of the wire neatly.

STEP 7. Open the jump ring with the round-nose and flat-nose pliers and attach the wire and beads to one of the ribbon clasps.

STEP 8. Repeat steps 3–7 with the other piece of wire and crystal beads to finish your bookmark.

7

AURA WAND

DIFFICULTY ◆ ◆ ◆

Crystal wands are used for cleansing the aura—a way of releasing blocked emotions and restoring calm and balance. Choose a crystal with a point to focus and channel energy through the wand. Think of this wand as an energetic paintbrush for cleansing.

You will need

Wand-shaped piece of wood (I used a local piece of willow)

Medium to large oblong crystal point

Hacksaw (optional)

2 x 1m (40in) pieces of 0.5mm (24 gauge) copper wire (for a wand approx. 35cm/14in long)

Fresh moss

Decorative beads (optional)

Pliers (round-nose, flat-nose and cutters)

Crystal choice

I chose smoky quartz for this aura wand because its earthiness complements the moss, and because the energy of this particular crystal is very grounding and calming. A crystal point works well to help direct and focus the energy through the wand. However, if you feel drawn to a smoother shape, don't be afraid to experiment: rounder edges have a gentler and softer energy and may be exactly what you need.

STEP 1. Part of the process of creating your wand is foraging and finding the perfect materials. Go out into a forest or woodland near you, and set the intention that you would like to find a piece of wood and some moss to create a crystal wand. Ask before you take anything, and give thanks to the earth when you do.

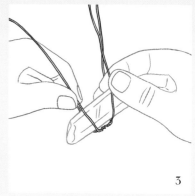

2

3

STEP 2. Cut the piece of wood to the desired length, if necessary. If you can get the angles of the edge of the crystal and wood to match, it will give a better flow for your wand and give the aesthetic that they have merged together naturally. You may need to sand or cut the wood to get a better fit.

STEP 3. Take the two wires, cross them over at the mid-point and twist them together at their middles until the twisted part is around 1cm (½in) long. Place the twisted wire against one side of your crystal.

STEP 4. You will have four wires around the side of your crystal. Take the two closest to the top of your crystal (not the end that will attach to the wand), twist them together so they fit snugly round the crystal, and make another twisted section down the crystal to create a symmetrical pattern.

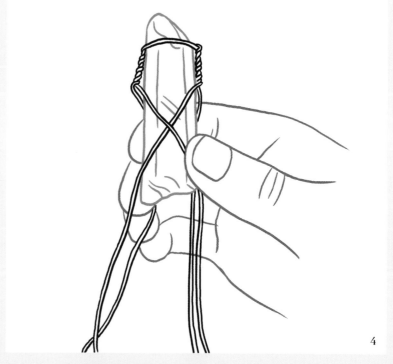

4

STEP 5. Take one wire from one twisted section, and one from the opposite twisted section, bring them together, and twist them to create a third twisted section. Repeat on the other side of the crystal. Continue wrapping the wires around the crystal in this way, making sure you get them as secure as you can.

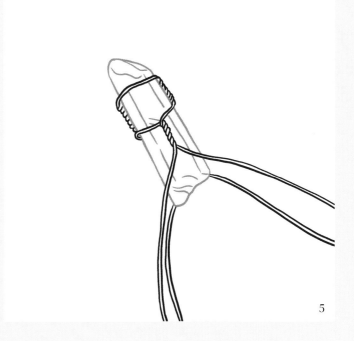

5

STEP 6. Break the moss into small pieces and put some between the crystal and the wooden wand. It may help to slightly dampen the moss as you work with it so that it has more flexibility.

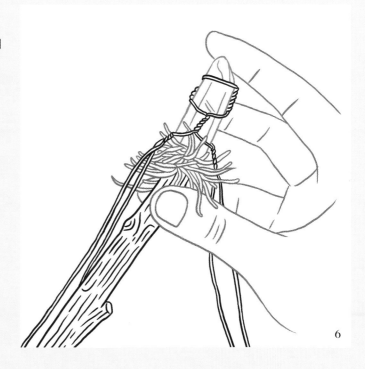

6

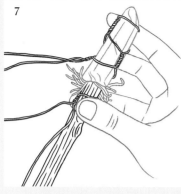

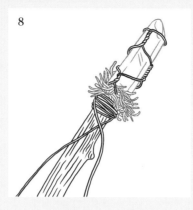

STEP 7. Continue wrapping the wires as before, moving down on to the wood. Make sure you are pulling the wires down and twisting them securely, as close to the wand as you can get.

STEP 8. Take two of the wires and lay them down the wand. Wrap the other two around the base of where the crystal and wood join, to give the crystal some extra security.

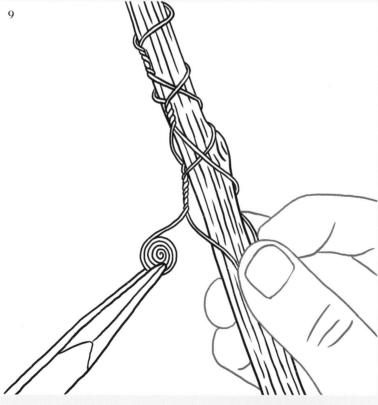

STEP 9. Keep wrapping the wire down the wood as before until you run out of wire. At this point, you could add some beads, or make patterns in the wire, such as coils or twists (as I have done here). Once you have used up all your wire, neatly tuck in any sharp edges with your pliers.

5   GRIDS &

INTENTIONS

MANIFESTATION GRID

DIFFICULTY ◆ ◆ ◆

Creating a crystal grid can be a great activity, even if you do not have a particular intention in mind: it can simply be a creative activity to connect with how different patterns and crystals feel and vibrate together. Working with the cycles of the moon can really support your manifesting power. A new moon is a good time to set new intentions.

You will need

Crystals in a selection of shapes and colors

Picture/sacred items/intentions for what you would like to manifest

Sacred geometric pattern (such as the flower of life), a grid, or cloth

Crystal choice

For this grid, I chose citrine, amethyst, and clear quartz points. Citrine can help attract more joyful, abundant energy. My intention for this grid was to amplify joy and creativity in my life. Points are a great shape for grids as they direct and send energy in the direction in which you point them—so, in a grid, you can send the energy in every direction!

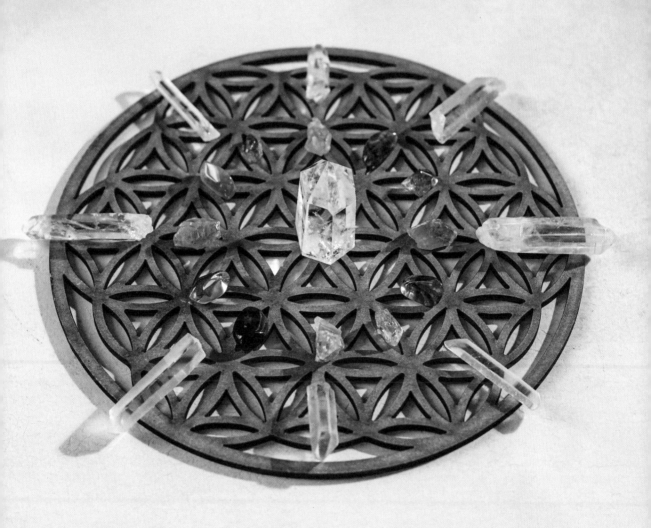

Let your heart
speak and your mind
conjure up the reality
of your intentions

STEP 1. The purpose of a manifestation grid is to align yourself with what you would like to create, experience, or attract in your life. The first step is to feel what it would be like to already have it. Close your eyes, take a couple of deep, cleansing breaths, and begin to visualize and sense what would be different in your life if your vision was already real. Let your heart speak and your mind conjure up the reality of what you can see, touch, smell, and feel in this vision. This is the key to unlock and manifest your desire into your reality.

STEP 2. Stay connected to your vision and choose the crystals you feel drawn to for your grid. If you have a photo or an object that helps represent your desire, you can also place this somewhere in your grid. When choosing your crystals, play with what feels good and where they seem to "fit." I like to use a combination of round crystals (for flow and a gentle energy) and some quartz points (which feel, to me, like crystal energy arrows shooting my vision out to the universe!).

STEP 3. Set up the space where you would like to create your grid. It's important that your grid is undisturbed for as long as you feel it needs to be in place, which could be a few days, a few weeks, or a moon cycle, depending on what you are seeking. Cleanse the space and maybe light a candle; whatever helps you bring some reverence and presence to your process.

STEP 4. Begin laying the crystals on your grid. I usually start with a central crystal and work outwards. You could also start from the outside and work in. This is a unique creation to you, so go with your intuition.

STEP 5. Once you feel happy with the pattern and feel of the grid, it is complete. Take some time to contemplate and give thanks for the crystals and the manifestation. Whenever you feel like you would like to reconnect to your vision, you can look at the grid, feel it, and let the universe take care of the rest. It's important to be patient and to not get too attached to a specific outcome. Trust what you feel and receive from the crystals and remember that you will attract the same energy you send out.

MEMORY JAR

DIFFICULTY ◆ ◇ ◇

Crystallize your memories and keep track of your favorite moments with this sacred jar. You could intentionally create this project on a birthday; as a new chapter in your life begins, you can record all of the best moments of the previous year and the things you are proud of. You could also create one for a friend with memories that you have shared together. By storing intentions and memories, any time you are facing a challenging period, you can recall all of these wonderful memories and trust that there will be more to come.

You will need

Pieces of paper

Pens

Ribbons and strings, to tie up the scrolls and decorate

Petals or a piece of fabric (to soften the bottom of the jar for your crystals)

Glass jar

Cleansed crystals of your choice

Paint pen, to decorate your jar (optional)

Crystal choice

I added a piece of rose quartz and carnelian to this jar with the intention to store and amplify fond memories of shared experiences.

STEP 1. Cut some pieces of paper into strips and write your memories, accomplishments, and favorite moments on them. Roll them up: you could use a pen or pencil to wrap them up neatly like little scrolls. You could also tie them with a small piece of string or ribbon to keep them together.

STEP 2. Place some petals or fabric in the bottom of the jar to create a nice, soft surface for your crystals. I added some rose petals here; they have a beautiful, soft texture and infuse the jar with a sweet, floral scent. You could use lavender, sage, or any other dried flower or herb you like.

STEP 3. Intentionally connect with your crystals and what you would like to create with this jar. Think about using this jar to memorialize moments in your life, and to hope for more moments of happiness in the future. Place your crystals in the jar. This is also the moment to add in any other special objects you would like, along with your rolled up memories.

STEP 4. Decorate the jar with paint pens, ribbons, or anything else that makes it feel special for you!

Try combining your best memories and proudest achievements from the past with your hopes and desires for the future to make a memory jar that will support you in your intentions through both good times and challenging ones. Filled with your personal crystal allies, this is one powerful object!

A MEMORY TO BE PROUD OF

AN AFFIRMATION FOR JOYFUL FUTURE EXPERIENCES

A HEARTWARMING
CHILDHOOD MEMORY

A WORK ACHIEVEMENT
YOU ARE PROUD OF

A MEMORABLE TIME SPENT
WITH A GOOD FRIEND

AN AFFIRMATION TO ATTRACT
A LOVING RELATIONSHIP

A MEMORY FROM YOUR TRAVELS

AN AFFIRMATION FOR
CHANGE IN THE FUTURE

EARTH
GRID

DIFFICULTY ◆ ◆ ◆

Creating a grid for the earth is a lovely way to connect to nature. If you go for a walk in the forest or at the beach, you will find an abundance of natural materials to add to your grid. You can leave a grid as an offering, with an intention to give love to the earth in a creative way.

You will need
A selection of crystals for your grid

Items from nature, such as leaves, petals, twigs, acorns, shells, etc.

Any other sacred objects you would like to incorporate

Crystal choice
I created this crystal grid with the intention of giving love and appreciation to the earth. I used selenite, rose quartz, smoky quartz, carnelian, and quartz crystal points. The cleansing selenite is at the center of this grid, and various shapes of rose quartz connect to the feminine energy of Mother Earth. You can use any combination of crystals you feel drawn to. Dedicate some time to connecting with the earth and giving thanks for all of the wonderful crystals she shares with us.

STEP 1. Go for walk in nature. You might be at home, exploring your local area, or on holiday: anywhere you can get creative and find natural items to make your grid is perfect. Look around and notice how much abundance nature gives us. Take a moment to feel and connect to any intention or idea you may want to create. Is there a particular reason you would like to make this grid? Is there a particular offering you have for the earth? Is it a full moon or new moon ritual?

STEP 2. Gather some natural items that you feel drawn to. Always ask permission before you take anything and try to only pick what has already fallen to the ground. I would not recommend cutting flowers or plants that are still alive; we want to create and give back in harmony with nature, not take what is growing and flourishing.

STEP 3. Start laying out the basic shape of your grid. Do you want to start with a circle or a square shape? Maybe start with a central object or crystal and build an outward spiral from that point. Make your grid however you want. Be guided by your intuition and remember that you can always change it if something doesn't look or feel right.

STEP 4. Keep building layers and patterns until you feel the grid is complete. Different shapes create different flows of energy: for example, a crystal point will be more dynamic and emphasize a direction, whereas if you choose to use round shapes, it will have a softer feel.

STEP 5. Once you have finished your grid, you may wish to take some moments to look at it, contemplate how it feels, and give thanks to the earth for these amazing crystals and the power of nature. You could place your hands over the crystals and visualize energy from the palm of your hands "activating" the grid and sending your love to the earth through your crystal grid.

6 TAKING

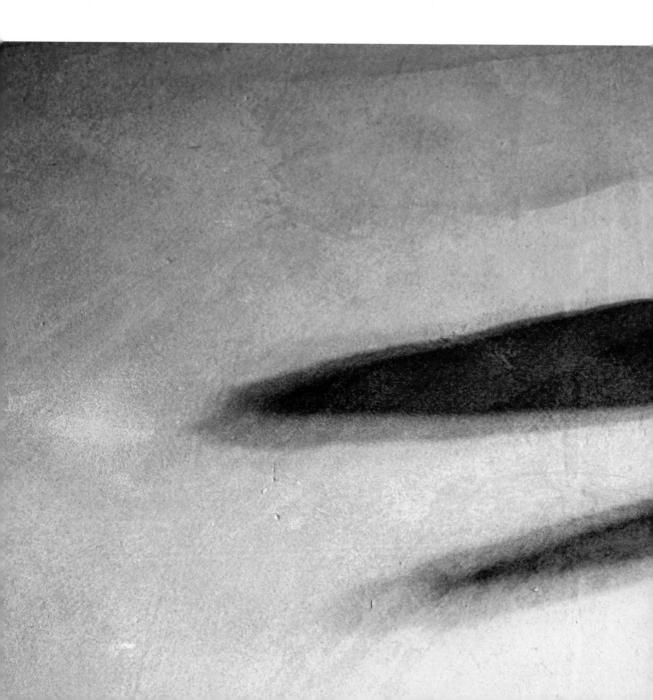

IT FURTHER

Crystals & Moon Power

If you live near the ocean, you might notice the waves become choppy during the full moon. The same thing is happening within us: the moon, whose energy rules our emotions, is stirring our internal waters.

As the moon waxes and wanes through her 28-day cycle, she illuminates different energies in our lives. Follow your inner guidance to connect with the different energies of the moon, creating rituals and crystal crafts. Remember to honor and give thanks to the moon, the earth, and the crystals you choose!

● New Moon

The new moon is the phase when the moon is dark and we can't see it. The moon is being reborn: it is the completion of the last cycle and the beginning of the next 28-day cycle. This is a great time to think about new beginnings—releasing the things you no longer want in your life, as well as sowing the seeds for future endeavors.

On a new moon, why not try making a crystal-enhanced bath potion (see page 100) and having a good, relaxing soak that will cleanse your mind as well as your body, allowing you to reset. Or you could try making a piece of jewelery—some earrings (see page 64), a pendant (see page 76), or a ring (see page 68)—that will focus and remind you of your intentions when you wear them.

◑ Waxing Moon

As the moon grows or waxes, this is the time to think about things you want to grow and nurture in your life—starting a new career, creating a deeper friendship with someone, or planning a new project, for example.

Try making a manifestation grid (see page 126) to amplify your intentions with the power of the waxing moon and crystals! It's also a perfect time to direct your love and attention towards others by making a gift such as a crystal pouch (see page 110) or a bookmark (see page 114) full of good wishes.

◯ Full Moon

The full moon can be an illuminating force in our lives, bringing us the strength and clarity we need to make empowering (and sustainable) personal changes. However, it can sometimes play havoc with our emotions, so beware of rushing into major decisions!

When you see the bright full moon in the sky, it is a time to celebrate our achievements and appreciate the moon's energy and guidance. Spend some time meditating on all the things you are thankful for or proud of by making a memory jar (see page 130). It is also a wonderful time to express your creative energies by making some artwork (see page 40) and for connecting with nature by giving your plants some love with a beautiful macramé plant hanger (see page 50) or making an earth grid (see page 134). The full moon is also a great time to cleanse your crystals and let them absorb the moon's light and wisdom.

◑ Waning Moon

As the moon wanes and winds down, so can you. This is a period for release and letting go of things, rather than calling new things into your life. Think about areas of your life you have been wanting to make changes, habits you've been hoping to drop, or any heaviness you are ready to release.

Cleanse your spirit and your skin during the waning moon by making yourself a detoxifying face mask (see page 96). You could make this a weekly self-care ritual, backed up with some crystal-infused water to help cleanse and detoxify (see page 104), and even an aura wand (see page 118) to support you in cleansing your home, your aura, and release any blocked and heavy energy from your life with crystal clear intentions.

Crystals & the Elements

Connecting the elements with your crystals, projects, and rituals can enhance the transformative power of your intentions. Each element has a different quality which you can connect to support different aspects of your life.

Ether

Ether is the subtlest element, also referred to as space. Call upon this element when you would like to focus on mindfulness, consciousness, the source of life, and acceptance. Crystals that can support you to connect with Ether are any tektite crystals (formed by meteorite impacts) and amethyst.

Earth

Earth is a grounding and stabilizing energy that you can call upon when you feel the need for connection to the physical world, to rest, feel physically strong, ground your energy, and find balance. Dark-colored crystals such as hematite or malachite connect with the earth element.

Air

Air is the opposite of earth: it is light and represents the mind and creativity. Call upon the element of air when you need to find fresh inspiration, or to focus on travel or communication. Amethyst and citrine are good choices to connect with this element.

Fire

Fire is an element that can both create and destroy. I like to connect with this element for new/full moon rituals, and I also call on fire to burn and transmute anything I am ready to release from my life. Deep orange and red crystals such as carnelian can connect with this element.

Water

Water is the element of emotion. We can connect with it when we are focusing on relationships and our spiritual skills. Water is also cleansing and purifying, and can help with healing. Selenite is a perfect crystal to connect with the energy of water.

Resources

I hope that this book has given you new ways to think about crystals and to bring crystal energy into your life. If you're inspired to learn more about crystals, here are some resources I recommend:

Books about Crystals

The Crystal Bible by Judy Hall
Crystals by Katie-Jane Wright
The Book of Stones: Who They Are and What They Teach by Robert Simmons and Naisha Ahsian
The Crystal Healing Guide by Simon Lilly

Websites about Crystals

Crystalfaqs.com
Lovelunalife.co.uk

Ethical Crystal Sellers

Kacha-stones.com
Energymuse.com
Sheslostcontrol.co.uk (check out the page about responsible mining)
thislavishearth.com

Crystal extraction and selling is currently not a well-regulated market, so it can be difficult to find ethical sellers. That's why it's so important to ask suppliers where their crystals come from. For the same reason, I highly recommend finding your own wild crystals where possible, and building a community of people to share crystals with. If you would like to know more, the website below has some interesting info about ethics (it can be translated to English through your browser or an online service): Fairtrademinerals.de

If you've enjoyed the projects in this book, why not learn more about crafting? Macramé and jewelery-making are especially good skills to learn for working with crystals, but you can bring crystals into any craft you can think of. Crafting on its own is a wonderfully mindful activity that comes with the added benefit that you can use and enjoy the results of your time. I recommend everyone to give it a go and find a craft they enjoy!

Acknowledgments

In memory of Marion Field. I am forever grateful for crossing paths with such a kindred spirit: you helped guide me to change the course of my life!

Thank you, Mother Earth, for everything you generously share with us. Thank you, crystals, for helping me unlock my potential, and for your healing energy, you have been companions and guides throughout some of the most challenging times of my life. Thank you, source, for the infinite energy, love, and healing that has guided me to be here now.

Thank you to my family. Thank you to my parents, Gayner and Tony, for your love and your encouragement to do what makes me truly happy and follow my heart. Thank you to my sisters, Katey and Amy: you both have been guardian angels throughout my life and mean the world to me. Thank you for your support and for always being there for me. Thank you, Enzo, for being an unconditional light in my life.

Thank you to all of my friends and teachers, past, present, and future, for believing in me, showing me support and love: you have been the sunshine that helped me to bloom and I am truly grateful for you. You know who you are, all you many beautiful souls all across the world!

A special thank you to Ellie Corbett and everyone who worked with me to create this beautiful book. Thank you to my ancestors and all those who came before me who sacrificed so much in order to make this life possible.

Thank you to every client who has supported me and seen the passion and love I put into my work, for your faith in me and kind words, you have given me so much faith in myself.

Thank YOU, for reading this book, for trusting yourself, opening up to the possibility that there is a whole world of magick at your fingertips. Keep listening to the silent wisdom of crystals!